A FIRST BOOK IN ALGEBRA

WALLACE C. BOYDEN, A.M.

HAWK PRESS

Published by

Hawk Press
4836/24, Ansari Road, Daryaganj
New Delhi – 110 002
Phones : 9643330713, + 91-11-23278618, + 91-11-35676207
E-mail : thehawkpress@gmail.com
www.thehawkpress.com

ISBN : 978-93-93971-57-9

A FIRST BOOK IN ALGEBRA

PREFACE

In preparing this book, the author had especially in mind classes in the upper grades of grammar schools, though the work will be found equally well adapted to the needs of any classes of beginners.

The ideas which have guided in the treatment of the subject are the following: The study of algebra is a continuation of what the pupil has been doing for years, but it is expected that this new work will result in a knowledge of *general truths* about numbers, and an increased power of clear thinking. All the differences between this work and that pursued in arithmetic may be traced to the introduction of two new elements, namely, negative numbers and the representation of numbers by letters. The solution of problems is one of the most valuable portions of the work, in that it serves to develop the thought-power of the pupil at the same time that it broadens his knowledge of numbers and their relations. Powers are developed and habits formed only by persistent, long-continued practice.

Accordingly, in this book, it is taken for granted that the pupil knows what he may be reasonably expected to have learned from his study of arithmetic; abundant practice is given in the representation of numbers by letters, and great care is taken to make clear the meaning of the minus sign as applied to a single number, together with the modes of operating upon negative numbers; problems are given in every exercise in the book; and, instead of making a statement of what the child is to see in the illustrative example, questions are asked which shall lead him to find for himself that which he is to learn from the example.

BOSTON, MASS., December, 1893.

Contents

A FIRST BOOK IN ALGEBRA.

ALGEBRAIC NOTATION.

1. Algebra is so much like arithmetic that all that you know about addition, subtraction, multiplication, and division, the signs that you have been using and the ways of working out problems, will be very useful to you in this study. There are two things the introduction of which really makes all the difference between arithmetic and algebra. One of these is the use of *letters to represent numbers*, and you will see in the following exercises that this change makes the solution of problems much easier.

Exercise I.

Illustrative Example. The sum of two numbers is 60, and the greater is four times the less. What are the numbers?

Solution.

Let	$x=$ the less number;
then	$4x=$ the greater number,
and	$4x+x=60$,
or	$5x=60$;
therefore	$x=12$,
and	$4x=48$. The numbers are 12 and 48.

1. The greater of two numbers is twice the less, and the sum of the numbers is 129. What are the numbers?

2. A man bought a horse and carriage for $500, paying three times as much for the carriage as for the horse. How much did each cost?

3. Two brothers, counting their money, found that together they had $186, and that John had five times as much as Charles. How much had each?

4. Divide the number 64 into two parts so that one part shall be seven times the other.

5. A man walked 24 miles in a day. If he walked twice as far in the forenoon as in the afternoon, how far did he walk in the afternoon?

6. For 72 cents Martha bought some needles and thread, paying eight times as much for the thread as for the needles. How much did she pay for each?

7. In a school there are 672 pupils. If there are twice as many boys as girls, how many boys are there?

Illustrative Example. If the difference between two numbers is 48, and one number is five times the other, what are the numbers?

Solution.

Let	$x=$ the less number;
then	$5x=$ the greater number,
and	$5x-x=48$,
or	$4x=48$;
therefore	$x=12$,
and	$5x=60$.

The numbers are 12 and 60.

8. Find two numbers such that their difference is 250 and one is eleven times the other.

9. James gathered 12 quarts of nuts more than Henry gathered. How many did each gather if James gathered three times as many as Henry?

10. A house cost $2880 more than a lot of land, and five times the cost of the lot equals the cost of the house. What was the cost of each?

11. Mr. A. is 48 years older than his son, but he is only three times as old. How old is each?

12. Two farms differ by 250 acres, and one is six times as large as the other. How many acres in each?

13. William paid eight times as much for a dictionary as for a rhetoric. If the difference in price was $6.30, how much did he pay for each?

14. The sum of two numbers is 4256, and one is 37 times as great as the other. What are the numbers?

15. Aleck has 48 cents more than Arthur, and seven times Arthur's money equals Aleck's. How much has each?

16. The sum of the ages of a mother and daughter is 32 years, and the age of the mother is seven times that of the daughter. What is the age of each?

17. John's age is three times that of Mary, and he is 10 years older. What is the age of each?

Exercise 2.

Illustrative Example. There are three numbers whose sum is 96; the second is three times the first, and the third is four times the first. What are the numbers?

Solution.

$$\begin{aligned} \text{Let} \qquad x &= \text{first number}, \\ 3x &= \text{second number}, \\ 4x &= \text{third number}. \\ x + 3x + 4x &= 96 \\ 8x &= 90 \\ x &= 12 \\ 3x &= 36 \\ 4x &= 48 \end{aligned}$$

The numbers are 12, 36, and 48.

1. A man bought a hat, a pair of boots, and a necktie for $7.50; the hat cost four times as much as the necktie, and the boots cost five times as much as the necktie. What was the cost of each?

2. A man traveled 90 miles in three days. If he traveled twice as far the first day as he did the third, and three times as far the second day as the third, how far did he go each day?

3. James had 30 marbles. He gave a certain number to his sister, twice as many to his brother, and had three times as many left as he gave his sister. How many did each then have?

4. A farmer bought a horse, cow, and pig for $90. If he paid three times as much for the cow as for the pig, and five times as much for the horse as for the pig, what was the price of each?

5. A had seven times as many apples, and B three times as many as C had. If they all together had 55 apples, how many had each?

6. The difference between two numbers is 36, and one is four times the other. What are the numbers?

7. In a company of 48 people there is one man to each five women. How many are there of each?

8. A man left $1400 to be distributed among three sons in such a way that James was to receive double what John received, and John double what Henry received. How much did each receive?

9. A field containing 45,000 feet was divided into three lots so that the second lot was three times the first, and the third twice the second. How large was each lot?

10. There are 120 pigeons in three flocks. In the second there are three times as many as in the first, and in the third as many as in the first and second combined. How many pigeons in each flock?

11. Divide 209 into three parts so that the first part shall be five times the second, and the second three times the third.

12. Three men, A, B, and C, earned \$110; A earned four times as much as B, and C as much as both A and B. How much did each earn?

13. A farmer bought a horse, a cow, and a calf for \$72; the cow cost twice as much as the calf, and the horse three times as much as the cow. What was the cost of each?

14. A cistern, containing 1200 gallons of water, is emptied by two pipes in two hours. One pipe discharges three times as many gallons per hour as the other. How many gallons does each pipe discharge in an hour?

15. A butcher bought a cow and a lamb, paying six times as much for the cow as for the lamb, and the difference of the prices was \$25. How much did he pay for each?

16. A grocer sold one pound of tea and two pounds of coffee for \$1.50, and the price of the tea per pound was three times that of the coffee. What was the price of each?

17. By will Mrs. Cabot was to receive five times as much as her son Henry. If Henry received \$20,000 less than his mother, how much did each receive?

Exercise 3.

Illustrative Example. Divide the number 126 into two parts such that one part is 8 more than the other.

Solution

Let x=less part,

$$x + 8 = \text{greater part.}$$
$$x + x + 8 = 126$$
$$2x + 8 = 126$$
$$2x = 118$$ [1]
$$x = 59$$
$$x + 8 = 67$$

The parts are 59 and 67.

1. In a class of 35 pupils there are 7 more girls than boys. How many are there of each?

[1] Where in arithmetic did you learn the principle applied in transposing the 8?

2. The sum of the ages of two brothers is 43 years, and one of them is 15 years older than the other. Find their ages.

3. At an election in which 1079 votes were cast the successful candidate had a majority of 95. How many votes did each of the two candidates receive?

4. Divide the number 70 into two parts, such that one part shall be 26 less than the other part.

5. John and Henry together have 143 marbles. If I should give Henry 15 more, he would have just as many as John. How many has each?

6. In a storehouse containing 57 barrels there are 3 less barrels of flour than of meal. How many of each?

7. A man whose herd of cows numbered 63 had 17 more Jerseys than Holsteins. How many had he of each?

8. Two men whose wages differ by 8 dollars receive both together $44 per month. How much does each receive?

9. Find two numbers whose sum is 99 and whose difference is 19.

10. The sum of three numbers is 56; the second is 3 more than the first, and the third 5 more than the first. What are the numbers?

11. Divide 62 into three parts such that the first part is 4 more than the second, and the third 7 more than the second.

12. Three men together received $34,200; if the second received $1500 more than the first, and the third $1200 more than the second, how much did each receive?

13. Divide 65 into three parts such that the second part is 17 more than the first part, and the third 15 less than the first.

14. A man had 95 sheep in three flocks. In the first flock there were 23 more than in the second, and in the third flock 12 less than in the second. How many sheep in each flock?

15. In an election, in which 1073 ballots were cast, Mr. A receives 97 votes less than Mr. B, and Mr. C 120 votes more than Mr. B. How many votes did each receive?

16. A man owns three farms. In the first there are 5 acres more than in the second and 7 acres less than in the third. If there are 53 acres in all the farms together, how many acres are there in each farm?

17. Divide 111 into three parts so that the first part shall be 16 more than the second and 19 less than the third.

18. Three firms lost $118,000 by fire. The second firm lost $6000 less than the first and $20,000 more than the third. What was each firm's loss?

Exercise 4.

Illustrative Example. The sum of two numbers is 25, and the larger is 3 less than three times the smaller. What are the numbers?

Solution.

$$\begin{aligned} \text{Let} \qquad x &= \text{smaller number,} \\ 3x-3 &= \text{larger number.} \\ x+3x-3 &= 25 \\ 4x-3 &= 25 \\ 4x &= 28^{2} \\ x &= 7 \\ 3x-3 &= 18 \end{aligned}$$

The numbers are 7 and 18.

1. Charles and Henry together have 49 marbles, and Charles has twice as many as Henry and 4 more. How many marbles has each?

2. In an orchard containing 33 trees the number of pear trees is 5 more than three times the number of apple trees. How many are there of each kind?

3. John and Mary gathered 23 quarts of nuts. John gathered 2 quarts more than twice as many as Mary. How many quarts did each gather?

4. To the double of a number I add 17 and obtain as a result 147. What is the number?

5. To four times a number I add 23 and obtain 95. What is the number?

6. From three times a number I take 25 and obtain 47. What is the number?

7. Find a number which being multiplied by 5 and having 14 added to the product will equal 69.

8. I bought some tea and coffee for \$10.39. If I paid for the tea 61 cents more than five times as much as for the coffee, how much did I pay for each?

9. Two houses together contain 48 rooms. If the second house has 3 more than twice as many rooms as the first, how many rooms has each house?

   Illustrative Example. Mr. Y gave \$6 to his three boys. To the second he gave 25 cents more than to the third, and to the first three times as much as to the second. How much did each receive?

Solution.

[2] Is the same principle applied here that is applied on page 12?

Let x=number of cents third boy received,

$x + 25$=number of cents second boy received,

$3x + 75$=number of cents first boy received.

$$x + x + 25 + 3x + 75 = 600$$
$$5x + 100 = 600$$
$$5x = 500$$
$$x = 100$$
$$x + 25 = 125$$
$$3x + 75 = 375$$

1st boy received \$3.75,
2d boy received \$1.25,
3d boy received \$1.00.

10. Divide the number 23 into three parts, such that the second is 1 more than the first, and the third is twice the second.

11. Divide the number 137 into three parts, such that the second shall be 3 more than the first, and the third five times the second.

12. Mr. Ames builds three houses. The first cost \$2000 more than the second, and the third twice as much as the first. If they all together cost \$18,000, what was the cost of each house?

13. An artist, who had painted three pictures, charged \$18 more for the second than the first, and three times as much for the third as the second. If he received \$322 for the three, what was the price of each picture?

14. Three men, A, B, and C, invest \$47,000 in business. B puts in \$500 more than twice as much as A, and C puts in three times as much as B. How many dollars does each put into the business?

15. In three lots of land there are 80,750 feet. The second lot contains 250 feet more than three times as much as the first lot, and the third lot contains twice as much as the second. What is the size of each lot?

16. A man leaves by his will \$225,000 to be divided as follows: his son to receive \$10,000 less than twice as much as the daughter, and the widow four times as much as the son. What was the share of each?

17. A man and his two sons picked 25 quarts of berries. The older son picked 5 quarts less than three times as many as the younger son, and the father picked twice as many as the older son. How many quarts did each pick?

18. Three brothers have 574 stamps. John has 15 less than Henry, and Thomas has 4 more than John. How many has each?

Exercise 5

.

Illustrative Example. Arthur bought some apples and twice as many oranges for 78 cents. The apples cost 3 cents apiece, and the oranges 5 cents apiece. How many of each did he buy?

Solution.

$$
\begin{aligned}
\text{Let}\qquad x &= \text{number of apples,}\\
2x &= \text{number of oranges,}\\
3x &= \text{cost of apples,}\\
10x &= \text{cost of oranges.}\\
3x + 10x &= 78\\
13x &= 78\\
x &= 6\\
2x &= 12
\end{aligned}
$$

Arthur bought 6 apples and 12 oranges.

1. Mary bought some blue ribbon at 7 cents a yard, and three times as much white ribbon at 5 cents a yard, paying $1.10 for the whole. How many yards of each kind did she buy?

2. Twice a certain number added to five times the double of that number gives for the sum 36. What is the number?

3. Mr. James Cobb walked a certain length of time at the rate of 4 miles an hour, and then rode four times as long at the rate of 10 miles an hour, to finish a journey of 88 miles. How long did he walk and how long did he ride?

4. A man bought 3 books and 2 lamps for $14. The price of a lamp was twice that of a book. What was the cost of each?

5. George bought an equal number of apples, oranges, and bananas for $1.08; each apple cost 2 cents, each orange 4 cents, and each banana 3 cents. How many of each did he buy?

6. I bought some 2-cent stamps and twice as many 5-cent stamps, paying for the whole $1.44. How many stamps of each kind did I buy?

7. I bought 2 pounds of coffee and 1 pound of tea for $1.31; the price of a pound of tea was equal to that of 2 pounds of coffee and 3 cents more. What was the cost of each per pound?

8. A lady bought 2 pounds of crackers and 3 pounds of gingersnaps for $1.11. If a pound of gingersnaps cost 7 cents more than a pound of crackers, what was the price of each?

9. A man bought 3 lamps and 2 vases for \$6. If a vase cost 50 cents less than 2 lamps, what was the price of each?

10. I sold three houses, of equal value, and a barn for \$16,800. If the barn brought \$1200 less than a house, what was the price of each?

11. Five lots, two of one size and three of another, aggregate 63,000 feet. Each of the two is 1500 feet larger than each of the three. What is the size of the lots?

12. Four pumps, two of one size and two of another, can pump 106 gallons per minute. If the smaller pumps 5 gallons less per minute than the larger, how much does each pump per minute?

13. Johnson and May enter into a partnership in which Johnson's interest is four times as great as May's. Johnson's profit was \$4500 more than May's profit. What was the profit of each?

14. Three electric cars are carrying 79 persons. In the first car there are 17 more people than in the second and 15 less than in the third. How many persons in each car?

15. Divide 71 into three parts so that the second part shall be 5 more than four times the first part, and the third part three times the second.

16. I bought a certain number of barrels of apples and three times as many boxes of oranges for \$33. I paid \$2 a barrel for the apples, and \$3 a box for the oranges. How many of each did I buy?

17. Divide the number 288 into three parts, so that the third part shall be twice the second, and the second five times the first.

18. Find two numbers whose sum is 216 and whose difference is 48.

Exercise 6

Illustrative Example. What number added to twice itself and 40 more will make a sum equal to eight times the number?

Solution.

$$\begin{aligned} \text{Let} \quad x &= \text{the number.} \\ x + 2x + 40 &= 8x \\ 3x + 40 &= 8x \\ 40 &= 5x \\ 8 &= x \end{aligned}$$

The number is 8.

1. What number, being increased by 36, will be equal to ten times itself?

2. Find the number whose double increased by 28 will equal six times the number itself.

3. If John's age be multiplied by 5, and if 24 be added to the product, the sum will be seven times his age. What is his age?

4. A father gave his son four times as many dollars as he then had, and his mother gave him $25, when he found that he had nine times as many dollars as at first. How many dollars had he at first?

5. A man had a certain amount of money; he earned three times as much the next week and found $32. If he then had eight times as much as at first, how much had he at first?

6. A man, being asked how many sheep he had, said, "If you will give me 24 more than six times what I have now, I shall have ten times my present number." How many had he?

7. Divide the number 726 into two parts such that one shall be five times the other.

8. Find two numbers differing by 852, one of which is seven times the other.

9. A storekeeper received a certain amount the first month; the second month he received $50 less than three times as much, and the third month twice as much as the second month. In the three months he received $4850. What did he receive each month?

10. James is 3 years older than William, and twice James's age is equal to three times William's age. What is the age of each?

11. One boy has 10 more marbles than another boy. Three times the first boy's marbles equals five times the second boy's marbles. How many has each?

12. If I add 12 to a certain number, four times this second number will equal seven times the original number. What is the original number?

13. Four dozen oranges cost as much as 7 dozen apples, and a dozen oranges cost 15 cents more than a dozen apples. What is the price of each?

14. Two numbers differ by 6, and three times one number equals five times the other number. What are the numbers?

15. A man is 2 years older than his wife, and 15 times his age equals 16 times her age. What is the age of each?

16. A farmer pays just as much for 4 horses as he does for 6 cows. If a cow costs 15 dollars less than a horse, what is the cost of each?

17. What number is that which is 15 less than four times the number itself?

18. A man bought 12 pairs of boots and 6 suits of clothes for \$168. If a suit of clothes cost \$2 less than four times as much as a pair of boots, what was the price of each?

Exercise 7

.

Illustrative Example. Divide the number 72 into two parts such that one part shall be one-eighth of the other.

Solution.

$$\begin{aligned} \text{Let} \qquad x &= \text{greater part,} \\ \tfrac{1}{8}x &= \text{lesser part.} \\ x + \tfrac{1}{8}x &= 72 \\ \tfrac{9}{8}x &= 72 \\ \tfrac{1}{8}x &= 8 \\ x &= 64 \end{aligned}$$

The parts are 64 and 8.

1. Roger is one-fourth as old as his father, and the sum of their ages is 70 years. How old is each?
2. In a mixture of 360 bushels of grain, there is one-fifth as much corn as wheat. How many bushels of each?
3. A man bought a farm and buildings for \$12,000. The buildings were valued at one-third as much as the farm. What was the value of each?
4. A bicyclist rode 105 miles in a day. If he rode one-half as far in the afternoon as in the forenoon, how far did he ride in each part of the day?
5. Two numbers differ by 675, and one is one-sixteenth of the other. What are the numbers?
6. What number is that which being diminished by one-seventh of itself will equal 162?
7. Jane is one-fifth as old as Mary, and the difference of their ages is 12 years. How old is each?

   Illustrative Example. The half and fourth of a certain number are together equal to 75. What is the number?

Solution.

$$\begin{aligned} \text{Let} \qquad x &= \text{the number.} \\ \tfrac{1}{2}x + \tfrac{1}{4}x &= 75. \\ \tfrac{3}{4}x &= 75 \\ \tfrac{1}{4}x &= 25 \\ x &= 100 \end{aligned}$$

The number is 100.

8. The fourth and eighth of a number are together equal to 36. What is the number?

9. A man left half his estate to his widow, and a fifth to his daughter. If they both together received \$28,000, what was the value of his estate?

10. Henry gave a third of his marbles to one boy, and a fourth to another boy. He finds that he gave to the boys in all 14 marbles. How many had he at first?

11. Two men own a third and two-fifths of a mill respectively. If their part of the property is worth \$22,000, what is the value of the mill?

12. A fruit-seller sold one-fourth of his oranges in the forenoon, and three-fifths of them in the afternoon. If he sold in all 255 oranges, how many had he at the start?

13. The half, third, and fifth of a number are together equal to 93. Find the number.

14. Mr. A bought one-fourth of an estate, Mr. B one-half, and Mr. C one-sixth. If they together bought 55,000 feet, how large was the estate?

15. The wind broke off two-sevenths of a pine tree, and afterwards two-fifths more. If the parts broken off measured 48 feet, how high was the tree at first?

16. A man spaded up three-eighths of his garden, and his son spaded two-ninths of it. In all they spaded 43 square rods. How large was the garden?

17. Mr. A's investment in business is \$15,000 more than Mr. B's. If Mr. A invests three times as much as Mr. B, how much is each man's investment?

18. A man drew out of the bank \$27, in half-dollars, quarters, dimes, and nickels, of each the same number. What was the number?

Exercise 8

Illustrative Example. What number is that which being increased by one-third and one-half of itself equals 22?

Solution.

$$\begin{aligned} \text{Let} \qquad x &= \text{the number.} \\ x + \tfrac{1}{3}x + \tfrac{1}{2}x &= 22. \\ 1\tfrac{5}{6}x &= 22 \\ \tfrac{11}{6}x &= 22 \\ \tfrac{1}{6}x &= 2 \\ x &= 12 \end{aligned}$$

The number is 12.

1. Three times a certain number increased by one-half of the number is equal to 14. What is the number?
2. Three boys have an equal number of marbles. John buys two-thirds of Henry's and two-fifths of Robert's marbles, and finds that he then has 93 marbles. How many had he at first?
3. In three pastures there are 42 cows. In the second there are twice as many as in the first, and in the third there are one-half as many as in the first. How many cows are there in each pasture?
4. What number is that which being increased by one-half and one-fourth of itself, and 5 more, equals 33?
5. One-third and two-fifths of a number, and 11, make 44. What is the number?
6. What number increased by three-sevenths of itself will amount to 8640?
7. A man invested a certain amount in business. His gain the first year was three-tenths of his capital, the second year five-sixths of his original capital, and the third year $3600. At the end of the third year he was worth $10,000. What was his original investment?
8. Find the number which, being increased by its third, its fourth, and 34, will equal three times the number itself.
9. One-half of a number, two-sevenths of the number, and 31, added to the number itself, will equal four times the number. What is the number?
10. A man, owning a lot of land, bought 3 other lots adjoining, – one three-eighths, another one-third as large as his lot, and the third containing 14,000 feet, – when he found that he had just twice as much land as at first. How large was his original lot?
11. What number is doubled by adding to it two-fifths of itself, one-third of itself, and 8?
12. There are three numbers whose sum is 90; the second is equal to one-half of the first, and the third is equal to the second plus three times the first. What are the numbers?
13. Divide 84 into three parts, so that the third part shall be one-third of the second, and the first part equal to twice the third plus twice the second part.
14. Divide 112 into four parts, so that the second part shall be one-fourth of the first, the third part equal to twice the second plus three times the first, and the fourth part equal to the second plus twice the first part.

15. A grocer sold 62 pounds of tea, coffee, and cocoa. Of tea he sold 2 pounds more than of coffee, and of cocoa 4 pounds more than of tea. How many pounds of each did he sell?

16. Three houses are together worth six times as much as the first house, the second is worth twice as much as the first, and the third is worth $7500. How much is each worth?

17. John has one-ninth as much money as Peter, but if his father should give him 72 cents, he would have just the same as Peter. How much money has each boy?

18. Mr. James lost two-fifteenths of his property in speculation, and three-eighths by fire. If his loss was $6100, what was his property worth?

Exercise 9

1. Divide the number 56 into two parts, such that one part is three-fifths of the other.

2. If the sum of two numbers is 42, and one is three-fourths of the other, what are the numbers?

3. The village of C—- is situated directly between two cities 72 miles apart, in such a way that it is five-sevenths as far from one city as from the other. How far is it from each city?

4. A son is five-ninths as old as his father. If the sum of their ages is 84 years, how old is each?

5. Two boys picked 26 boxes of strawberries. If John picked five-eighths as many as Henry, how many boxes did each pick?

6. A man received 60-1/2 tons of coal in two carloads, one load being five-sixths as large as the other. How many tons in each carload?

7. John is seven-eighths as old as James, and the sum of their ages is 60 years. How old is each?

8. Two men invest $1625 in business, one putting in five-eighths as much as the other. How much did each invest?

9. In a school containing 420 pupils, there are three-fourths as many boys as girls. How many are there of each?

10. A man bought a lot of lemons for $5; for one-third he paid 4 cents apiece, and for the rest 3 cents apiece. How many lemons did he buy?

11. A lot of land contains 15,000 feet more than the adjacent lot, and twice the first lot is equal to seven times the second. How large is each lot?

12. A bicyclist, in going a journey of 52 miles, goes a certain distance the first hour, three-fifths as far the second hour, one-half as far the third hour, and 10 miles the fourth hour, thus finishing the journey. How far did he travel each hour?

13. One man carried off three-sevenths of a pile of loam, another man four-ninths of the pile. In all they took 110 cubic yards of earth. How large was the pile at first?

14. Matthew had three times as many stamps as Herman, but after he had lost 70, and Herman had bought 90, they put what they had together, and found that they had 540. How many had each at first?

15. It is required to divide the number 139 into four parts, such that the first may be 2 less than the second, 7 more than the third, and 12 greater than the fourth.

16. In an election 7105 votes were cast for three candidates. One candidate received 614 votes less, and the other 1896 votes less, than the winning candidate. How many votes did each receive?

17. There are four towns, A, B, C, and D, in a straight line. The distance from B to C is one-fifth of the distance from A to B, and the distance from C to D is equal to twice the distance from A to C. The whole distance from A to D is 72 miles. Required the distance from A to B, B to C, and C to D.

MODES OF REPRESENTING THE OPERATIONS.

ADDITION.

2. ILLUS. 1. The sum of $y + y + y +$ etc. written seven times is $7y$.

ILLUS. 2. The sum of $m + m + m +$ etc. written x times is xm.

The 7 and x are called the coefficients of the number following.

The **coefficient** is the number which shows how many times the number following is taken additively. If no coefficient is expressed, *one* is understood.

Read each of the following numbers, name the coefficient, and state what it shows:

$$6a,\ 2y,\ 3x,\ ax,\ 5m,\ 9c,\ xy,\ mn,\ 10z,\ a,\ 25n,\ x,\ 11xy.$$

ILLUS. 3. If John has x marbles, and his brother gives him 5 marbles, how many has he?

ILLUS. 4. If Mary has x dolls, and her mother gives her y dolls, how many has she?

Addition is expressed by coefficient and by sign plus(+). When use the coefficient? When the sign?

Exercise 10.

1. Charles walked x miles and rode 9 miles. How far did he go?
2. A merchant bought a barrels of sugar and p barrels of molasses. How many barrels in all did he buy?
3. What is the sum of $b + b + b +$ etc. written eight times?
4. Express the, sum of x and y.
5. There are c boys at play, and 5 others join them. How many boys are there in all?
6. What is the sum of $x + x + x +$ etc. written d times?
7. A lady bought a silk dress for m dollars, a muff for l dollars, a shawl for v dollars, and a pair of gloves for c dollars. What was the entire cost?
8. George is x years old, Martin is y, and Morgan is z years. What is the sum of their ages?
9. What is the sum of m taken b times?
10. If d is a whole number, what is the next larger number?
11. A boy bought a pound of butter for y cents, a pound of meat for z cents, and a bunch of lettuce for s cents. How much did they all cost?
12. What is the next whole number larger than m?
13. What is the sum of x taken y times?
14. A merchant sold x barrels of flour one week, 40 the next week, and a barrels the following week. How many barrels did he sell?
15. Find two numbers whose sum is 74 and whose difference is 18.

SUBTRACTION.

3. ILLUS. 1. A man sold a horse for \$225 and gained \$75. What did the horse cost?

ILLUS. 2. A farmer sold a sheep for m dollars and gained y dollars. What did the sheep cost? *Ans.* $m - y$ dollars.

Subtraction is expressed by the sign minus $(-)$.

ILLUS. 3. A man started at a certain point and traveled north 15 miles, then south 30 miles, then north 20 miles, then north 5 miles, then south 6 miles. How far is he from where he started and in which direction?

ILLUS. 4. A man started at a certain point and traveled east x miles, then west b miles, then east m miles, then east y miles, then west z miles. How far is he from where he started?

We find a difficulty in solving this last example, because we do not know just how large x, b, m, y, and z are with reference to each other. This is only one example of a large class of problems which may arise, in which we find direction east and west, north and south; space before and behind, to the right and to the left, above and below; time past and future; money gained and lost; everywhere these opposite relations. This relation of oppositeness must be expressed in some way in our representation of numbers.

In algebra, therefore, numbers are considered as increasing from zero in opposite directions. Those in one direction are called Positive Numbers (or + numbers); those in the other direction Negative Numbers (or - numbers).

In Illus. 4, if we call direction east positive, then direction west will be negative, and the respective distances that the man traveled will be $+x$, $-b$, $+m$, $+y$, and $-z$. Combining these, the answer to the problem becomes $x-b+m+y-z$. If the same analysis be applied to Illus. 3, we get 15 - 30 + 20 + 5 - 6 = +4, or 4 miles north of starting-point.

The minus sign before a single number makes the number negative, and shows that the number has a subtractive relation to any other to which it may be united, and that it will diminish that number by its value. It shows a relation rather than an operation.

Negative numbers are the second of the two things referred to on page 7, the introduction of which makes all the difference between arithmetic and algebra.

NOTE.—Negative numbers are usually spoken of as less than zero, because they are used to represent losses. To illustrate: suppose a man's money affairs be such that his debts just equal his assets, we say that he is worth nothing. Suppose now that the sum of his debts is \$1000 greater than his total assets. He is worse off than by the first supposition, and we say that he is worth less than nothing. We should represent his property by -1000 (dollars).

Exercise 11.

1. Express the difference between a and b.

2. By how much is b greater than 10?

3. Express the sum of a and b diminished by c.

4. Write five numbers in order of magnitude so that a shall be the middle number.

5. A man has an income of a dollars. His expenses are b dollars. How much has he left?

6. How much less than c is 8?

7. A man has four daughters each of whom is 3 years older than the next younger. If x represent the age of the oldest, what will represent the age of the others?

8. A farmer bought a cow for b dollars and sold it for c dollars. How much did he gain?

9. How much greater than 5 is x?

10. If the difference between two numbers is 9, how may you represent the numbers?

11. A man sold a house for x dollars and gained \$75. What did the house cost?

12. A man sells a carriage for m dollars and loses x dollars. What was the cost of the carriage?

13. I paid c cents for a pound of butter, and f cents for a lemon. How much more did the butter cost than the lemon?

14. Sold a lot of wood for b dollars, and received in payment a barrel of flour worth e dollars. How many dollars remain due?

15. A man sold a cow for l dollars, a calf for 4 dollars, and a sheep for m dollars, and in payment received a wagon worth x dollars. How much remains due?

16. A box of raisins was bought for a dollars, and a firkin of butter for b dollars. If both were sold for c dollars, how much was gained?

17. At a certain election 1065 ballots were cast for two candidates, and the winning candidate had a majority of 207. How many votes did each receive?

18. A merchant started the year with m dollars; the first month he gained x dollars, the next month he lost y dollars, the third month he gained b dollars, and the fourth month lost z dollars. How much had he at the end of that month?

19. A man sold a cow for \$80, and gained c dollars. What did the cow cost?

20. If the sum of two numbers is 60, how may the numbers be represented?

MULTIPLICATION

4. ILLUS. 1. $4 \cdot 5 \cdot a \cdot b \cdot c$, 7×6, $x \times y$.

ILLUS. 2. abc, xy, amx.

ILLUS. 3. $x \cdot x = xx = x^2$.
$x \cdot x \cdot x = xxx = x^3$.

These two are read "x second power," or "x square," and "x third power," or "x cube," and are called powers of x.

A **power** is a product of like factors.

The 2 and the 3 are called the exponents of the power.

An **exponent** is a number expressed at the right and a little above another number to show how many times it is taken as a factor.

Multiplication is expressed (1) by signs, i.e. the dot and the cross; (2) by writing the factors successively; (3) by exponent.

The last two are the more common methods.

When use the exponent? When write the factors successively?

Exercise 12

1. Express the double of x.

2. Express the product of x, y, and z.

3. How many cents in x dollars?

4. Write a times b times c.

5. What will a quarts of cherries cost at d cents a quart?

6. If a stage coach, goes b miles an hour, how far will it go in m hours?

7. In a cornfield there are x rows, and a hills in a row. How many hills in the field?

8. Write the cube of x.

9. Express in a different way $a \times a \times a \times a \times a \times a \times a \times a \times a$.

10. Express the product of a factors each equal to d.

11. Write the second power of a added to three times the cube of m.

12. Express x to the power $2m$, plus x to the power m.

13. What is the interest on x dollars for m years at 6 %?

14. In a certain school there are c girls, and three times as many boys less 8. How many boys, and how many boys and girls together?

15. If x men can do a piece of work in 9 days, how many days would it take 1 man to perform the same work?

16. How many thirds are there in x?

17. How many fifths are there in b?

18. A man bought a horse for x dollars, paid 2 dollars a week for his keeping, and received 4 dollars a week for his work. At the expiration of a weeks he sold him for m dollars. How much did he gain?

19. James has a walnuts, John twice as many less 8, and Joseph three times as many as James and John less 7. How many have all together?

DIVISION

5. ILLUS. $a \div b$, $\frac{x}{y}$

Division is expressed by the division sign, and by writing the numbers in the fractional form.

Exercise 13

1. Express five times a divided by three times c.

2. How many dollars in y cents?

3. How many books at a dimes each can be bought for x dimes?

4. How many days will a man be required to work for m dollars if he receive y dollars a day?

5. x dollars were given for b barrels of flour. What was the cost per barrel?

6. Express a plus b, divided by c.

7. Express a, plus b divided by c.

8. A man had a sons and half as many daughters. How many children had he?

9. If the number of minutes in an hour be represented by x, what will express the number of seconds in 5 hours?

10. A boy who earns b dollars a day spends x dollars a week. How much has he at the end of 3 weeks?

11. A can perform a piece of work in x days, B in y days, and C in z days. Express the part of the work that each can do in one day. Express what part they can all do in one day.

12. How many square feet in a garden a feet on each side?

13. A money drawer contains a dollars, b dimes, and c quarters. Express the whole amount in cents.

14. x is how many times y?

15. If m apples are worth n chestnuts, how many chestnuts is one apple worth?

16. Divide 30 apples between two boys so that the younger may have two-thirds as many as the elder.

ALGEBRAIC EXPRESSIONS.

6. ILLUS. $a,\ -c,\ b+8,\ m-x+2c^2$.

An **algebraic expression** is any representation of a number by algebraic notation.

7. ILLUS. 1. $-3a^2b,\ 2x+a^2z^3-5d^4$.

$-3a^2b$ is called a term, $2x$ is a term, $+a^2z^3$ is a term, $-5d^4$ is a term.

A **term** is an algebraic expression not connected with any other by the sign plus or minus, or one of the parts of an algebraic expression with its own sign plus or minus. If no sign is written, the plus sign is understood. By what signs are terms separated?

ILLUS. 2.

$$\begin{array}{cc} a^2bc & 3x^2y^3 \\ -7a^2bc & -x^2y^3 \\ 5a^2bc & \frac{1}{2}x^2y^3 \end{array}$$

The terms in these groups are said to be similar.

ILLUS. 3.

$$\begin{array}{ccc} x^2y & xy & x^2y \\ 3a^2b & 3x^2y & 3ab \end{array}$$

The terms of these groups are said to be dissimilar.

Similar terms are terms having the same letters affected by the same exponents.

Dissimilar terms are terms which differ in letters or exponents, or both.

How may similar terms differ?

ILLUS. 4.

$abxy$....fourth degree....$7x^2y^2$

x^3.... third degree ....abc

$3xy$....second degree....a^2

$2a^2bx^3$.... sixth degree ....$4a^5b$

The **degree of a term** is the number of its literal factors. It can be found by taking the sum of its exponents.

ILLUS. 5. $2x^4$
$-a^3y$
$5x^2y^2$

How do these terms compare with reference to degree? They are called *homogeneous* terms.

What are homogeneous terms?

8. ILLUS. $3x^2y$ called a monomial.

$$\left.\begin{array}{l} 7x^3 - 2xy \\ 3y^4 - z^2 \quad +3yz^2 \end{array}\right\} \text{ called polynomials.}$$

A **monomial** is an algebraic expression of one term.

A **polynomial** is an algebraic expression of more than one term.

A polynomial of two terms is called a **binomial**, and one of three terms is called a **trinomial.**

The **degree of an algebraic expression** is the same as the degree of its highest term. What is the degree of each of the polynomials above? What is a homogeneous polynomial?

Exercise 14.

1. Write a polynomial of five terms. Of what degree is it?
2. Write a binomial of the fourth degree.
3. Write a polynomial with the terms of different degrees.
4. Write a homogeneous trinomial of the third degree.
5. Write two similar monomials of the fifth degree which shall differ as much as possible.
6. Write a homogeneous trinomial with one of its terms of the second degree.
7. Arrange according to the descending powers of a: $-80a^3b^3 + 60a^4b^2 + 108ab^5 + 48a^5b + 3a^6 - 27b^6 - 90a^2b^4$.

   What name? What degree?
8. Write a polynomial of the fifth degree containing six terms.
9. Arrange according to the ascending powers of x:

$$15x^2y^3 + 7x^5 - 3xy^5 - 60x^4y + y^7 + 21x^3y^2$$

What name? What degree? What is the degree of each term?

When $a = 1$, $b = 2$, $c = 3$, $d = 4$, $x = O$, $y = 8$, find the value of the following:

10. $2a + 3b + c$.

11. $5b + 3a - 2c + 6x$.

12. $6bc - 3ax + 2xb - 5ac + 2cx$.

13. $3bcd + 5cxa - 7xab + abc$.

14. $2c^2 + 3b^3 + 4a^4$.

15. $\frac{1}{2}a^3c - b^3 - c^3 - \frac{3}{4}abc^3$.

16. $2a - b - \frac{2ab}{a+b}$.

17. $2bc - \frac{3}{4}c^3 + 3ab - 2a - x + \frac{4}{15}bx$.

18. $\frac{a^2bx+ab^2c+abc^2+xac^2}{abc}$.

19. Henry bought some apples at 3 cents apiece, and twice as many pears at 4 cents apiece, paying for the whole 66 cents. How many of each did he buy?

20. Sarah's father told her that the difference between two-thirds and five-sixths of his age was 6 years. How old was he?

OPERATIONS.

ADDITION.

9. In combining numbers in algebra it must always be borne in mind that negative numbers are the opposite of positive numbers in their tendency.

ILLUS. 1.

$$\begin{array}{rr} 3ax & -7b^2y \\ 5ax & -3b^2y \\ 2ax & -4b^2y \\ \hline 10ax & -14b^2y \end{array}$$

To add similar terms with like signs, add the coefficients, annex the common letters, and prefix the common sign.

ILLUS. 2.

$$\begin{array}{rr} 5a^2b & 3x^2y^2 \\ -3a^2b & 8x^2y^2 \\ -4a^2b & -5x^2y^2 \\ 6a^2b & -7x^2y^2 \\ \hline 4a^2b & -x^2y^2 \end{array}$$

To add similar terms with unlike signs, add the coefficients of the plus terms, add the coefficients of the minus terms, to the difference of these sums annex the common letters, and prefix the sign of the greater sum.

ILLUS. 3.

$$\begin{array}{cc} a & 2x \\ b & -5y \\ c & -3a \\ \hline a+b+c & 2x-5-3a \end{array}$$

To add dissimilar terms, write the terms successively, each with its own sign.

ILLUS. 4.

$$\begin{array}{rrrr} 2ab & -3ax^2 & +2a^2x & \\ -8ab & -ax^2 & -5a^2x & +ax^3 \\ 12ab & +10ax^2 & -6a^2x & \\ \hline 6ab & +6ax^2 & -9a^2x & +ax^3 \end{array}$$

To add polynomials, add the terms of which the polynomials consist, and unite the results.

Exercise 15.

Find the sum of:

1. $3x$, $5x$, x, $4x$, $11x$.

2. $5ab$, $6ab$, ab, $13ab$.

3. $-3ax^3$, $-5ax^3$, $-9ax^3$, $-ax^3$.

4. $-x$, $-5x$, $-11x$, $-25x$.

5. $-2a^2$, $5a^2$, $3a^2$, $-7a^2$, $11a^2$.

6. $2abc^2$, $-5abc^2$, abc^2, $-8abc^2$.

7. $5x^2$, $3ab$, $-2ab$, $-4a^2$, $5ab$, $-2a^2$.

8. $5ax$, $-3bc$, $-2ax$, $7ax$, bc, $-2bc$.

Simplify:

9. $4a^2 - 5a^2 - 8a^2 - 7a^2$.

10. $x^5 + 5a^4b - 7ab - 2x^5 + 10ab + 3a^4b$.

11. $\frac{1}{3}a - \frac{1}{2}a + \frac{2}{3}a + a$.

12. $\frac{2}{3}b - \frac{3}{4}b - 2b - \frac{1}{3}b + \frac{5}{6}b + b$.

13. A lady bought a ribbon for m cents, some tape for d cents, and some thread for c cents. She paid x cents on the bill. How much remains due?

14. A man travels a miles north, then x miles south, then 5 miles further south, and then y miles north. How far is he from his starting point?

Add:

15. $a + 2b + 3c$, $5a + 3b + c$, $c - a - b$.

16. $x + y - z$, $x - y - z$, $y - x + z$.

17. $x + 2y - 3z + a$, $2x - 3y + z - 4a$, $2a - 3x + y - z$.

18. $x^3 + 3x^2 - x + 5$, $4x^2 - 5x^3 + 3 - 4x$, $3x + 6x^3 - 3x^2 + 9$.

19. $ca - bc + c^3$, $ab + b^3 - ca$, $a^3 - ab + bc$.

20. $3a^m - a^{m-1} - 1$, $3a^{m-1} + 1 - 2a^m$, $a^{m-1} + 1$.

21. $5a^5 - 16a^4b - 11a^2b^2c + 13ab$, $-2a^5 + 4a^4b + 12a^2b^2c - 10ab$, $6a^5 - a^4b - 6a^2b^2c + 10ab$, $-10a^5 + 8a^4b + a^2b^2c - 6ab$, $a^5 + 5a^4b + 6a^2b^2c - 7ab$.

22. $15x^3 + 35x^2 + 3x + 7$, $7x^3 + 15x - 11x^2 + 9$, $9x - 10 + x^3 - 4x^2$.

23. $9x^5y - 6x^4y^2 + x^3y^3 - 25xy^5$, $-22x^3y^3 - 3xy^5 - 9x^5y - 3x^4y^2$, $5x^3y^3 + x^5y + 21x^4y^2 + 20xy^5$.

24. $x-y-z-a-b$, $x+y+z+a+b$, $x+y+z+a-b$, $x+y-z-a-b$, $x+y+z-a-b$.

25. $a^2c+b^2c+c^3-abc-bc^2-ac^2$, $a^2b+b^3-bc^2-ab^2-b^2c-abc$, $a^3+ab^2+ac^2-a^2b-abc-a^2c$.

26. A regiment is drawn up in m ranks of b men each, and there are c men over. How many men in the regiment?

27. A man had x cows and z horses. After exchanging 10 cows with another man for 19 horses, what will represent the number that he has of each?

28. In a class of 52 pupils there are 8 more boys than girls. How many are there of each?

What is the sum of two numbers equal numerically but of opposite sign? How does the sum of a positive and negative number compare in value with the positive number? with the negative number? How does the sum of two negative numbers compare with the numbers? Illustrate the above questions by a man traveling north and south.

SUBTRACTION.

10. How is subtraction related to addition? How are opposite relations expressed?

Given the typical series of numbers

$\mathbf{-4a, \ -3a, \ -2a, \ -a, \ -0, \ a, \ 2a, \ 3a, \ 4a, \ 5a.}$

What must be added to $2a$ to obtain $5a$? What then must be subtracted from $5a$ to obtain $2a$? $5a-3a=?$

What must be added to $-3a$ to obtain $4a$? What then must be subtracted from $4a$ to obtain $-3a$? $4a-7a=?$

What must be added to $3a$ to obtain $-2a$? What then must be subtracted from $-2a$ to obtain $3a$? $(-2a)-(-5a)=?$

What must be added to $-a$ to obtain $-4a$? What then must be subtracted from $-4a$ to obtain $-a$? $(-4a)-(-3a)=?$

Examine now these results expressed in another form.

$$\begin{array}{llrlr} 1. & \text{From} & 5a & \text{To} & 5a \\ & \text{take} & 3a & \text{add} & -3a \\ \cline{3-3}\cline{5-5} & & 2a & & 2a \end{array}$$

$$\begin{array}{llrlr} 2. & \text{From} & 4\text{a} & \text{To} & 4\text{a} \\ & \text{take} & 7a & \text{add} & -7a \\ \cline{3-3}\cline{5-5} & & -3a & & -3a \end{array}$$

$$\begin{array}{llrlr} 3. & \text{From} & 2a & \text{To} & 2a \\ & \text{take} & 5a & \text{add} & -5a \\ \cline{3-3}\cline{5-5} & & -3a & & -3a \end{array}$$

$$\begin{array}{llrlr} 4. & \text{From} & -4a & \text{To} & -4a \\ & \text{take} & -3a & \text{add} & 3a \\ \cline{3-3}\cline{5-5} & & -a & & -a \end{array}$$

The principle is clear; namely,

The subtraction of any number gives the same result as the addition of that number with the opposite sign.

ILLUS.

$$\begin{array}{r} 6a + 3b - c \\ -4a + b - 5c \\ \hline 10a + 2b + 4c \end{array}$$

To subtract one number from another, consider the sign of the subtrahend changed and add.

What is the relation of the minuend to the subtrahend and remainder? What is the relation of the subtrahend to the minuend and remainder?

Exercise 16.

1. From $5a^3$ take $3a^3$.
2. From $7a^2b$ take $-5a^2b$.
3. Subtract $7xy^3$ from $-2xy^3$.
4. From $-3x^my$ take $-7x^my$.
5. Subtract $3ax$ from $8x^2$.
6. From $5xy$ take $-7by$.
7. What is the difference between $4a^m$ and $2a^m$?
8. From the difference between $5a^2x$ and $-3a^2x$ take the sum of $2a^2x$ and $-3a^2x$.
9. From $2a + b + 7c$ take $5a + 2b - 7c$.
10. From $9x - 4y + 3z$ take $5x - 3y + z$.

11. Subtract $3x^4 - x^2 + 7x - 14$ from $11x^4 - 2x^3 - 8x$.

12. From $10a^2b^2 + 15ab^2 + 8a^2b$ take $-10a^2b^2 + 15ab^2 - 8a^2b$.

13. Subtract $1 - x + x^2 - 3x^3$ from $x^3 - 1 + x^2 - x$.

14. From $x^m - 2x^{2m} + x^{3m}$ take $2x^{3m} - x^{2m} - x^m$.

15. Subtract $a^{2n} + a^n x^n + x^{2n}$ from $3a^{2n} - 17a^n x^n - 8x^{2n}$.

16. From $\frac{2}{3}a^2 - \frac{5}{2}a - 1$ take $-\frac{2}{3}a^2 + a - \frac{1}{2}$.

17. From $x^5 + 3xy^4$ take $x^5 + 2x^4y + 3x^3y^2 - 2xy^4 + y^5$.

18. From x take $y - a$.

19. From $6a^3 + 4a + 7$ take the sum of $2a^3 + 4a^2 + 9$ and $4a^3 - a^2 + 4a - 2$.

20. Subtract $3x - 7x^3 + 5x^2$ from the sum of $2 + 8x^2 - x^3$ and $2x^3 - 3x^2 + x - 2$.

21. What must be subtracted from $15y^3 + z^3 + 4yz^2 - 5z^2x - 2xy^2$ to leave a remainder of $6x^3 - 12y^3 + 4z^3 - 2xy^2 + 6z^2x$?

22. How much must be added to $x^3 - 4x^2 + 16x$ to produce $x^3 + 64$?

23. To what must $4a^2 - 6b^2 + 8bc - 6ab$ be added to produce zero?

24. From what must $2x^4 - 3x^2 + 2x - 5$ be subtracted to produce unity?

25. What must be subtracted from the sum of $3a^3 + 7a + 1$ and $2a^2 - 5a - 3$ to leave a remainder of $2a^2 - 2a^3 - 4$?

26. From the difference between $10a^2b + 8ab^2 - 8a^2b^2 - b^3$ and $5a^2b - 6ab^3 - 7a^2b^2$ take the sum of $10a^2b^2 + 15ab^2 + 8a^2b$ and $8a^2b - 5ab^2 + a^2b^2$.

27. What must be added to a to make b?

28. By how much does $3x - 2$ exceed $2x + 1$?

29. In y years a man will be 40 years old. What is his present age?

30. How many hours will it take to go 23 miles at a miles an hour?

PARENTHESES

11. ILLUS. 1. $5(a + b)$.
ILLUS. 2. $(m + n)(x + y)$.
ILLUS. 3. $x - (a + y - c)$.

The parenthesis indicates that the numbers enclosed are considered as one number.

Read each of the above illustrations, state the operations expressed, and show what the parenthesis indicates.

Write the expressions for the following:

1. The sum of a and b, multiplied by a minus b.

2. c plus d, times the sum of a and b,—the whole multiplied by x minus y.

3. The sum of a and b, minus the difference between two a and three b.

4. $(x - y) + (x - y) + (x - y) +$ etc., written a times.

5. The sum of $a + b$ taken seven times.

6. There are in a library $m + n$ books, each book has $c - d$ pages, and each page contains $x + y$ words. How many words in all the books?

ILLUS. 4. $a + (b - c - x) = a + b - c - x$.
(By performing the addition.)

ILLUS. 5. $a + c - d + e = a + (c - d + e)$.

Any number of terms may be removed from a parenthesis preceded by the plus sign without change in the terms.

And conversely,

Any number of terms may be enclosed in a parenthesis preceded by the plus sign without change in the terms.

ILLUS. 6. $x - (y + z - c) = x - y - z + c$.
(By performing the subtraction.)

ILLUS. 7. $a - b - c + d = a - (b + c - d)$.

Any number of terms may be removed from a parenthesis preceded by the minus sign by changing the sign of each term.

And conversely,

Any number of terms may be enclosed in a parenthesis preceded by the minus sign by changing the sign of each term.

Exercise 17

Remove the parentheses in the following:

1. $x + (a + b) + y + (c - d) + (x - y)$.

2. $a + (b - c) - b + (a + c) + (c - a)$.

3. $a^2b - (a^3 + b^3) - a^3 - (ab^2 - a^2b) - (b^3 - a^3)$.

4. $xy - (x^2 + y^2) - y^2 - (x^2 - 2xy) - (y^2 - x^2)$.

5. $(a + b - c) - (a - b + c) + (b - a - c) - (c - a - b)$.

6. $(x - y + z) + (x + y + z) - (y + x + z) - (z + x + y)$.

7. $a - (3b - 2c + a) - (2b - a - c) - (6 - c + a)$.

8. $\frac{1}{2}a - \frac{1}{2}c - (\frac{2}{3}b - \frac{1}{2}c) - (a + \frac{1}{4}c - \frac{1}{3}b) - (\frac{2}{3}b - \frac{1}{4}c - \frac{1}{2}a)$.

In each of the following enclose the last two terms in a parenthesis preceded by a plus sign:

9. $x - y + 2c - d$.

10. $2a^2 + 3a^3x - ab^2 + by^2$.

11. $10m^3 + 31m^2 - 20m - 21$.

12. $ax^4 - x^3 + 2x - 2ax^2$.

In each of the following enclose the last three terms in a parenthesis preceded by a minus sign:

13. $a^4 + a^3x + a^2x^2 - ax^3 - 4x^4$.

14. $a^4 + a^3 - 6a^2 + a + 3$.

15. $6a^3 - 17a^2x + 14ax^2 - 3x^3$.

16. $ax^3 + 2ax^2 + ax + 2a$.

17. A man pumps x gallons of water into a tank each day, and draws off y gallons each day. How much water will remain in the tank at the end of five days?

18. Two men are 150 miles apart, and approach each other, one at the rate of x miles an hour, the other at the rate of y miles an hour. How far apart will they be at the end of seven hours?

19. Eight years ago A was x years old. How old is he now?

20. A had x dollars, but after giving \$35 to B he has one-third as much as B. How much has B?

MULTIPLICATION.

12. ILLUS. 1.

$$\begin{array}{ll} 8 = 2 \cdot 2 \cdot 2 & \qquad a^3 = a \cdot a \cdot a \\ 6 = 2 \cdot 3 & \qquad b^2 = b \cdot b \\ \hline 48 = 2 \cdot 2 \cdot 2 \cdot 2 \cdot 3 & \qquad a^3b^2 = a \cdot a \cdot a \cdot b \cdot b \end{array}$$

ILLUS. 2.

$$\begin{array}{l} 2a^2b^3c \\ 3a^4b^2c^3 \\ \hline 6a^6b^5c^4 \end{array}$$

In arithmetic you learned that multiplication is the addition of equal numbers, that the multiplicand expresses one of those equal numbers, and the multiplier the number of them. In algebra we have negative as well as positive numbers. Let us see the effect of this in multiplication. We have four possible cases.

1. Multiplication of a plus number by a plus number.

$$\begin{array}{r} +7 \\ \underline{+4} \end{array}$$

ILLUS. This must mean *four sevens*, or 28.

2. Multiplication of a minus number by a plus number.

$$\begin{array}{r} -7 \\ \underline{+4} \end{array}$$

ILLUS. This must mean *four minus-sevens*, or -28.

3. Multiplication of a plus number by a minus number.

$$\begin{array}{r} +7 \\ \underline{-4} \end{array}$$

ILLUS. This must mean the opposite of what $+4$ meant as a multiplier. Plus four meant add, minus four must mean subtract. *Subtracting four sevens* gives -28.

4. Multiplication of a minus number by a minus number.

$$\begin{array}{r} -7 \\ \underline{-4} \end{array}$$

ILLUS. This must mean *subtract four minus-sevens*, or 28.

ILLUS. 3.

$$\begin{array}{cccc} +b & -b & +b & -b \\ \underline{+a} & \underline{+a} & \underline{-a} & \underline{-a} \\ ab & -ab & -ab & ab \end{array}$$

To multiply a monomial by a monomial, multiply the coefficients together for the coefficient of the product, add the exponents of like letters for the exponent of the same letter in the product, and give the product of two numbers having like signs the plus sign, having unlike signs the minus sign.

Exercise 18.

Find the product of:

1. $5x$ and $7c$.
2. $51cy$ and $-xa$.
3. $3x^3y$ and $7axy^2$.
4. $5a^2bc$ and $2ab^2c^3$.
5. $-3x^2y$, $-2ax$, and $3cy^2$.
6. $5a^2$, $-3bc^3$, and $-2abc$.
7. $15x^2y^2$, $-\frac{2}{3}xz$, and $\frac{1}{10}yz^2$.
8. $20a^3b^2$, $\frac{2}{5}ab^2$, and $-\frac{1}{8}bc^2$.
9. $\frac{1}{2}xy$, $-\frac{2}{3}cx^2$, $-\frac{2}{5}a^2y$, and $-\frac{5}{3}x^2y^2$.
10. $-\frac{2}{3}a^2b^2$, $\frac{1}{4}c^2$, $-\frac{6}{5}ac$, and $-\frac{3}{4}b^3c$.

11. In how many days will a boys eat 100 apples if each boy eats b apples a day?

12. How many units in x hundreds?

13. If there are a hundreds, b tens, and c units in a number, what will represent the whole number of units?

14. If the difference between two numbers is 7, and one of the numbers is x, what is the other number?

13. ILLUS. 1.

$$\begin{array}{r} a - b + c \\ x \\ \hline ax - bx + cx \end{array}$$

To multiply a polynomial by a monomial, multiply each term of the polynomial by the monomial, and add the results.

ILLUS. 2.

$$\begin{array}{r} x^3 + 2x^2 + 3x \qquad\qquad\quad \\ 3x^2 - 2x + 1 \qquad\qquad\quad \\ \hline 3x^5 + 6x^4 + 9x^3 \qquad\qquad\qquad\qquad \\ -2x^4 - 4x^3 - 6x^2 \qquad\qquad \\ x^3 + 2x^2 + 3x \\ \hline 3x^5 + 4x^4 + 6x^3 - 4x^2 + 3x \end{array}$$

To multiply a polynomial by a polynomial, multiply the multiplicand by each term of the multiplier, and add the products.

How is the first term of the product obtained? How is the last term obtained? The polynomials being arranged similarly with reference to the exponents of some number, how is the product arranged?

Exercise 19.

Multiply:

1. $x^2 + xy + y^2 \text{by} x^2y^2$.
2. $a^2 - ab + b^2 \text{by} a^2b$.
3. $a^3 - 3a^2b + b^3 \text{by} - 2ab$.
4. $8x^3 + 36x^2y + 27y^3 by 3xy^2$.
5. $\frac{5}{6}a^4 - \frac{1}{5}a^3b - \frac{1}{3}a^2b^2 \text{by} \frac{6}{5}ab^2$.
6. $x^2 - xy + y^2 \text{by} x + y$.
7. $x^4 - 3x^3 + 2x^2 - x + 1$ by $x - 1$.
8. $x^3 - 2x^2 + x$ by $x^2 + 3x + 1$.
9. $xy + mn - xm - yn$ by $xy - mn + xm - yn$.

10. $x^4 - x^3 + x^2 - x + 1$ by $2 + 3x + 2x^2 + x^3$.

11. $a^5 - a^4b + a^3b^2 - a^2b^3 + ab^4 - b^5$ by $a + b$.

12. $x^2 - xy + y^2 - yz + z^2 - xz$ by $x + y + z$.

13. $x^6 + x^5y + x^4y^2 + x^3y^3 + x^2y^4 + xy^5 + y^6$ by $x - y$.

14. $x^4 - 4a^2x^2 + 4a^4$ by $x^4 + 4a^2x^2 + 4a^4$.

15. $a^3 - 3a^2y^2 + y^3$ by $a^3 + 3a^2y^2 + y^3$.

16. $x^4 + 10x + 12 + 9x^2 + 3x^3$ by $-2x + x^2 - 1$.

17. $3x^2 - 2 + x^3 - 3x + 6x^4$ by $-2 + x^2 - 3x$.

18. If x represent the number of miles a man can row in an hour in still water, how far can the man row in 5 hours down a stream which flows y miles an hour? How far up the same stream in 4 hours?

19. A can reap a field in 7 hours, and B can reap the same field in 5 hours. How much of the field can they do in one hour, working together?

20. A tank can be filled by two pipes in a hours and b hours respectively. What part of the tank will be filled by both pipes running together for one hour?

What does $x - y$ express? What two operations will give that result? What operations will give $4x$ as a result?

14. ILLUS. 1.

$$\begin{array}{r} x + 5 \phantom{{}+15} \\ x + 3 \phantom{{}+15} \\ \hline x^2 + 5x \phantom{{}+15} \\ 3x + 15 \\ \hline x^2 + 8x + 15 \end{array}$$

ILLUS. 2.

$$\begin{array}{r} x - 5 \phantom{{}+15} \\ x - 3 \phantom{{}+15} \\ \hline x^2 - 5x \phantom{{}+15} \\ -\ 3x + 15 \\ \hline x^2 - 8x + 15 \end{array}$$

ILLUS. 3.

$$\begin{array}{r} x + 5 \phantom{{}-15} \\ x - 3 \phantom{{}-15} \\ \hline x^2 + 5x \phantom{{}-15} \\ -\ 3x - 15 \\ \hline x^2 + 2x - 15 \end{array}$$

ILLUS. 4.

$$\begin{array}{r@{}l} x - 5 & \\ x + 3 & \\ \hline x^2 - 5x & \\ 3x - 15 & \\ \hline x^2 - 2x - 15 & \end{array}$$

How many terms in the product? What is the first term? How is the last term formed? How is the coefficient of x in the middle term formed?

The answers to the examples in the following exercise are to be written directly, and not to be obtained by the full form of multiplication:

Exercise 20.

Expand:

1. $(x+2)(x+7)$.
2. $(x+1)(x+6)$.
3. $(x-3)(x-4)$.
4. $(x-5)(x-2)$.
5. $(x+5)(x-2)$.
6. $(x+7)(x-3)$.
7. $(x-7)(x+6)$.
8. $(x-6)(x+5)$.
9. $(x-11)(x-2)$.
10. $(x-13)(x-1)$.
11. $(y+7)(y-9)$.
12. $(x+3)(x+17)$.
13. $(y+2)(y-15)$.
14. $(y+2)(y+16)$.
15. $(a^2+7)(a^2-5)$.
16. $(a-9)(a+9)$.
17. $(m^2-2)(m^2-16)$.
18. $(b^3+12)(b^3-10)$.
19. $(x-\frac{1}{2})(x-\frac{1}{4})$.

20. $(y + \frac{1}{3})(y + \frac{1}{6})$.

21. $(m + \frac{2}{3})(m - \frac{1}{3})$.

22. $(a - \frac{2}{5})(a + \frac{3}{5})$.

23. $(x - \frac{2}{3})(x - \frac{1}{2})$.

24. $(y + \frac{3}{4})(y + \frac{1}{5})$.

25. $(3 - x)(7 - x)$.

26. $(5 - x)(3 - x)$.

27. $(6 - x)(7 + x)$.

28. $(11 - x)(3 + x)$.

29. $(x - 3)(x + 3)$.

30. $(y + 5)(y - 5)$.

31. Find a number which, being multiplied by 6, and having 15 added to the product, will equal 141.

32. Mr. Allen has 3 more cows than his neighbor. Three times his number of cows will equal four times his neighbor's. How many has Mr. Allen?

INVOLUTION.

15. What is the second power of 5? What is the third power of 4?

Involution is the process of finding a power of a number.

ILLUS. 1. $(5a^2b^3)^2 = 25a^4b^6$.

ILLUS. 2. $(3xy^2z)^3 = 27x^3y^6z^3$.

ILLUS. 3. Find by multiplication the 2d, 3d, 4th, and 5th powers of $+a$ and $-$ Observe the signs of the odd and of the even powers.

To find any power of a monomial, raise the coefficient to the required power, multiply the exponent of each letter by the exponent of the power, and give every even power the plus sign, every odd power the sign of the original number.

Exercise 21

.

Expand:

1. $(a^2b)^2$.

2. $(xy^2)^3$.

3. $(-a^4b)^2$.

4. $(-x^3y^2)^3$.

5. $(3a^2y)^3$.

6. $(-7ab^2c^3)^2$.

7. $(xyz^2)^5$.

8. $(-m^2nd)^4$.

9. $(-5x^3y^4z)^3$.

10. $(11c^5d^12x^4)^2$.

11. $(\frac{1}{2}x^2am^3)^2$.

12. $(-\frac{1}{3}ab^3c)^2$.

13. $(-15c^6dx^2)^2$.

14. $(-9xy^5z^2)^3$.

15. $(a^9b^2c^4d^2)^4$.

16. $(-x^8yz^3m^2n)^5$.

17. $(-\frac{2}{3}a^2bc^4)^2$.

18. $(\frac{5}{6}mn^2x^3)^2$.

19. In how many days can one man do as much as b men in 8 days?

20. How many mills in a cents? How many dollars?

16. Find by multiplication the following:

$$(a+b)^2,\ (a-b)^2,\ (a+b)^3,\ (a-b)^3,\ (a+b)^4,\ (a-b)^4.$$

Memorize the results.

It is intended that the answers in the following exercise shall be written directly without going through the multiplication.

ILLUS. 1. $(x-y)^4 = x^4 - 4x^3y + 6x^2y^2 - 4xy^3 + y^4$.
ILLUS. 2. $(x-1)^3 = x^3 - 3x^2 + 3x - 1$.

ILLUS. 3. $(2xy+3y^2)^4$

$$\begin{aligned} &= (2xy)^4 + 4(2xy)^3(3y^2) + 6(2xy)^2(3y^2)^2 \\ &\qquad + 4(2xy)(3y^2)^3 + (3y^2)^4 \\ &= 16x^4y^4 + 96x^3y^5 + 216x^2y^6 + 216xy^7 + 81y^8. \end{aligned}$$

Exercise 22.

Expand:

1. $(z + x)^3$.
2. $(a + y)^4$.
3. $(x - a)^4$.
4. $(a - m)^3$.
5. $(m + a)^2$.
6. $(x - y)^2$.
7. $(x^2 + y^2)^3$.
8. $(m^3 - y^2)^2$.
9. $(c^2 - d^2)^4$.
10. $(y^2 + z^4)^3$.
11. $(x^2y + z)^2$.
12. $(a^2b - c)^4$.
13. $(a^2 - b^3c)^3$.
14. $(x^2y - mn^3)^2$.
15. $(x + 1)^3$.
16. $(m - 1)^2$.
17. $(b^2 - 1)^4$.
18. $(y^3 + 1)^3$.
19. $(ab - 2)^2$.
20. $(x^2y - 3)^2$.
21. $(1 - x)^4$.
22. $(1 - y^2)^3$.
23. $(2x + 3y^2)^2$.
24. $(3ab - x^2y)^3$.
25. $(4mn^3 - 3a^2b)^4$.
26. $(\frac{1}{2}x - y)^2$.

27. $(1 - \frac{1}{3}x^2)^3$.

28. $(x^2 - 3)^4$.

29. John has $4a$ horses, James has a times as many as John, and Charles has d less than five times as many as James. How many has Charles?

30. A man bought a pounds of meat at a cents a pound, and handed the butcher an x-dollar bill. How many cents in change should he receive?

31. A grocer, having 25 bags of meal worth a cents a bag, sold x bags. What is the value of the meal left?

32. If $a = 5$, $x = 4$, $y = 3$, find the numerical value of

$$\frac{7a}{11x - 3y} + \frac{11x}{8x - 7y} - \frac{10y}{7a - 5x}.$$

33. Find the value of

$$a^2b - c^2d - (ab + cd)(ac - bd) - bc(a^2c - bd^2)$$

when $a = 2$, $b = 3$, $c = 4$, and $d = 0$.

Exercise 23. (Review.)

1. Take the sum of $x^3 + 3x - 2$, $2x^3 + x^2 - x + 5$, and $4x^3 + 2x^2 - 7x + 4$ from the sum of $2x^3 + 9x$ and $5x^3 + 3x^2$.
2. Multiply $b^4 - 2b^2$ by $b^4 + 2b^2 - 1$.
3. Simplify $11x^2 + 4y^2 - (2xy - 3y^2) + (2x^2 - 3xy) - (3x^2 - 5xy)$.
4. Divide \$300 among A, B, and C, so that A shall have twice as much as B, and B \$20 more than C.
5. Find two numbers differing by 8 such that four times the less may exceed twice the greater by 10.
6. What must be added to $3a^3 - 4a^2 - 4$ to produce $5a^3 + 6$?
7. Add $\frac{2}{3}a^2 - ab - \frac{5}{4}b^2$, $\frac{2}{3}a^2 + \frac{1}{3}ab - \frac{1}{4}b^2$, and $-a^2 - \frac{2}{3}ab + 2b^2$.
8. Simplify $8ab^2c^4 \times (-3a^4bc^2) \times (-2a^2b^3c)$.
9. Expand $\left(-\frac{2}{3}xy^2z^3\right)^4$.
10. Simplify $(x - 2)(x + 7) + (x - 8)(x - 5)$.
11. Expand $(2a^2b - 3xy)^3$.
12. What must be subtracted from $x^3 - 3x^2 + 2y - 5$ to produce unity?

13. Multiply $x^3 + 3x^2y + 3xy^2 + y^3$ by $3xy^2 - y^3 - 3x^2y + x^3$.

14. Expand $(x + 1)(x - 1)(x^2 + 1)$.

15. Add $4xy^3 - 4y^4$, $4x^3y - 12x^2y^2 + 12xy^3 - 4y^4$, $6x^2y^2 - 12xy^3 + 6y^4$ and $x^4 - 4x^3y + 6x^2y^2 - 4xy^3 + y^4$.

16. A man weighs 36 pounds more than his wife, and the sum of their weights is 317 pounds. What is the weight of each?

17. A watch and chain cost \$350. What was the cost of each, if the chain cost $\frac{3}{4}$ as much as the watch?

18. Simplify $3x^2 - 2x + 1 - (x^2 + 2x + 3) - (2x^2 - 6x - 6)$.

19. Simplify $(a + 2y)^2 - (a - 2y)^2$

20. What is the value of $1 + \frac{1}{2}a + \frac{1}{3}b$ times $1 - \frac{1}{2}a + \frac{1}{3}b$?

DIVISION.

17. What is the relation of division to multiplication?

ILLUS. $3x^2 \times 2xy =$? then $6x^3y \div 2xy =$?

Division is the process by which, when a product is given and one factor known, the other factor is found.

What is the relation of the dividend to the divisor and quotient? What factors must the dividend contain? What factors must the quotient contain?

ILLUS. 1. $6a^4b^4c^6 \div 2a^3b^2c^3 = 3ab^2c^3$.

ILLUS. 2. $+ab \underline{\big| +ab^2}$ $\quad -ab \underline{\big| +ab^2}$ $\quad +ab \underline{\big| -ab^2}$ $\quad -ab \underline{\big| -ab^2}$

From the relation of the dividend, divisor, and quotient, and the law for signs in multiplication, obtain the quotients in Illus. 2.

To divide a monomial by a monomial, divide the coefficient of the dividend by the coefficient of the divisor for the coefficient of the quotient, subtract the exponent of each letter in the divisor from the exponent of the same letter in the dividend for the exponent of that letter in the quotient: if dividend and divisor have like signs, give the quotient the plus sign; if unlike, the minus sign.

Exercise 24.

Divide:

1. $15x^2y$ by $3x$.

2. $39ab^2$ by $3b$.

3. $27a^3b^3c$ by $9ab^2c$.

4. $35x^4y^4z$ by $7x^2yz$.

5. $-51cx^3y$ by $3cyx^2$.

6. $121x^3y^3z$ by $-11y^2z$.

7. $-28x^2y^2z^2$ by $-7xy^2$.

8. $-36a^3b^2c^4$ by $-4ab^2c^2$.

9. $\frac{1}{3}a^4b^5$ by $\frac{1}{6}a^2b^2$.

10. $\frac{1}{5}x^3y^4$ by $-\frac{1}{15}xy^3$.

11. $-45x^5y^7z$ by $9x^2y^4z$.

12. $60a^4bc^{11}$ by $-4ab^2c^7$.

13. $-\frac{2}{3}x^7y^2$ by $-\frac{5}{6}x^4y$.

14. $\frac{3}{4}a^5m^4n^3$ by $-\frac{1}{4}a^2mn^3$.

15. $5m^4n^2x^5$ by $\frac{5}{8}mn^2x$.

16. $4x^3y^2z^8$ by $-\frac{2}{3}xz^5$.

17. $10(x+y)^4z^3$ by $5(x+y)^2z$.

18. $15(a-b)^3x^2$ by $3(a-b)x$.

19. Simplify $(-x^2y^3z^2) \times (-x^4y^5z^4) \div 2x^3y^3z^4$.

20. Simplify $a^5b^2c \times (-a^3b^3c^3) \div 3(a^3bc^2)^2$.

21. Expand $(x^3y^2 - 3xy)^3$.

22. If a man can ride one mile for a cents, how far can two men ride for b cents?

23. In how many days can x men earn as much as 8 men in y days?

24. a times b is how many times c?

18. ILLUS.

$$-3ab^3 \,\underline{\big|\; -6a^3b^3 \quad + \quad 15a^2b^4 \quad - \quad 3ab^5}$$
$$\qquad\qquad 2a^2 \quad - \quad 5ab \quad + \quad b^2$$

To divide a polynomial by a monomial, divide each term of the dividend by the divisor, and add the quotients.

Exercise 25.

Divide:

1. $18a^4b^3 - 42a^3b^2 + 90a^6bx$ by $6a^3b$.
2. $10x^5y^2 + 6x^3y^2 - 18x^4y^4$ by $2x^3y$.
3. $72x^5y^6 - 36x^4y^3 - 18x^2y^2$ by $9x^2y$.
4. $169a^4b - 117a^3b^2 + 91a^2b$ by $13a^2$.
5. $-2a^5x^3 + \frac{7}{2}a^4x^4$ by $\frac{7}{3}a^3x$.
6. $\frac{1}{2}x^5y^2 - 3x^3y^4$ by $-\frac{3}{2}x^3y^2$.
7. $32x^3y^4z^6 - 24x^5y^4z^4 + 8x^4y^2$ by $-8x^3y$.
8. $120a^4b^3c^5 - 186a^5b^7c^6$ by $6a^3b^3c^4$.
9. $4x^8 - 10x^5 + 2x^6 - 16x^3 - 6x^4$ by $4x^2$.
10. $24y^3 + 32y^7 - 48y^6$ by $3y^3$.
11. $\frac{1}{4}a^2x - \frac{1}{16}abx - \frac{3}{8}acx$ by $\frac{3}{8}ax$.
12. $-\frac{5}{2}x^2 + \frac{5}{3}xy + \frac{10}{3}x$ by $-\frac{5}{6}x$.
13. An army was drawn up with x men in front and y men deep. How many men were there in the army?
14. In how many minutes will a train go x miles at the rate of a miles an hour?
15. How many apples at x cents apiece can be bought for b dollars?

19. Since division is the reverse of multiplication, let us consider an example in the multiplication of polynomials.

$$\begin{array}{rrrrr}
x^3 & +\,2x^2 & +\,3x & & \\
3x^2 & -\,2x & +\,3 & & \\
\hline
3x^5 & +\,6x^4 & +\,9x^3 & & \\
 & -\,2x^4 & -\,4x^3 & -\,6x^2 & \\
 & & 3x^3 & +\,6x^2 & +\,9x \\
\hline
3x^5 & +\,4x^4 & +\,8x^3 & & +\,9x
\end{array}$$

Which of these numbers will become the dividend in our division? Take $x^3 + 2x^2 + 3x$ for the divisor. What will be the quotient? Write these names opposite the different numbers. What is the last operation performed in obtaining the dividend? What then is the dividend? How are these partial products obtained?

Keeping these facts in mind, we will start on the work of division, using these same numbers for convenience.

ILLUS. 1.[3]

$$
\begin{array}{rllll}
x^3+2x^2+3x) & 3x^5 +4x^4 + 8x^3 + 9x & (3x^2 -2x+3 \\
 & \underline{3x^5 +6x^4 + 9x^3} & \\
 & \quad -2x^4 - x^3 + 9x & \\
 & \quad \underline{-2x^4 - 4x^3 - 6x} & \\
 & \qquad\quad 3x^3 + 6x^2 +9x & \\
 & \qquad\quad 3x^3 + 6x^2 +9x &
\end{array}
$$

How was the first term of the dividend formed? How can the first term of the quotient be found? Knowing the divisor and first term of the quotient, what can be formed? Subtract this from the dividend. How was the first term of the remainder formed? What can now be found? How? What can then be formed? etc., etc. How long can this process be continued?

ILLUS. 2.

$$
\begin{array}{rll}
x^2-3xy+2y^2) & x^4 -6x^3y +12x^2y^2 -4y^4 & (x^2 \quad -3xy+y^2+\frac{9xy^3-6y^4}{x^2-3xy+2y^2} \\
 & \underline{x^4 -3x^3y \ +2x^2y^2} & \\
 & \quad -3x^3y +10x^2y^2 -4y^4 & \\
 & \quad \underline{-3x^3y \ +9x^2y^2 -6xy^3} & \\
 & \qquad\qquad x^2y^2 +6xy^3 -4y^4 & \\
 & \qquad\qquad \underline{x^2y^2 -3xy^3 +2y^4} & \\
 & \qquad\qquad\quad 9xy^3 \quad -6y^4 &
\end{array}
$$

Why stop the work at the point given? What is the complete quotient? Is the dividend exactly divisible by the divisor? When is one number exactly divisible by another?

To divide a polynomial by a polynomial, arrange the terms of the dividend, and divisor similarly, divide the first term of the dividend by the first term of the divisor for the first term of the quotient, multiply the divisor by the quotient and subtract the product from the dividend; divide the first term of the remainder by the first term of the divisor for the next term of the quotient, multiply and subtract as before; continue this work of dividing, multiplying, and subtracting until there is no remainder or until the first term of the remainder is not divisible by the first term of the divisor.

Exercise 26.

Divide:

1. $x^2+8x-105$ by $x+15$.
2. $x^2+8x-33$ by $x+11$.
3. x^4+x^2-20 by x^2-4.
4. y^4-y^2-30 by y^2+5.
5. x^4-31x^2+9 by x^2+5x-3.

[3]It would be well for the teacher to work out this example on the board with the class along the line of the questions which follow the example.

6. $a^4 - 12a^2 + 16$ by $a^2 - 2a - 4$.

7. $x^3 - y^3$ by $x - y$.

8. $a^3 + b^3$ by $a + b$.

9. $16a^4 - 81b^4$ by $2a - 3b$.

10. $81x^8 - y^4$ by $3x^2 - y$.

11. $x^5 - x^4y - 2x^3y^2 - 5x^2y^3 - 17xy^4 - 12y^5$ by $x^2 - 2xy - 3y^2$.

12. $a^5 + a^4b - 14a^3b^2 + 15a^2b^3 - 4b^3$ by $a^2 - 3ab + 2b^2$.

13. $x^6 - 5x^3 + 3 + 5x^4 - 10x - x^5 + 10x^2$ by $x^2 + 3 - x$.

14. $x^6 - 2x^3 - 2 + x - 3x^5 + 2x^4 - 5x^2$ by $x^3 + 2 + x$.

15. $a^5 - a - 2a^2 - a^3$ by $a + a^3 + a^2$.

16. $x^6 - 2x^3 - x^2 - x^4$ by $1 + xx^2 + x$.

17. $a^{11} - a^2$ by $a^3 - 1$.

18. $a^{12} - a^4$ by $a^2 + 1$.

19. $x^4 + 4y^4$ by $x^2 - 2xy + y^2$.

20. $4a^4 + 81b^4$ by $2a^2 + 6ab + 9b^2$.

21. $\frac{1}{2}x^4 + \frac{3}{4}x^3y - \frac{1}{3}x^2y^2 + \frac{7}{6}xy^3 - \frac{1}{3}y^4$ by $x^2 - \frac{1}{2}xy + y^2$.

22. $\frac{2}{9}y^3 - \frac{5}{36}x^2y + \frac{1}{6}xy^2 + \frac{1}{6}x^3$ by $\frac{1}{2}x + \frac{1}{3}y$.

23. $\frac{1}{4}(x-y)^5 - (x-y)^3 - \frac{1}{2}(x-y)^2 - \frac{1}{16}(x-y)$ by $\frac{1}{2}(x-y)^2 + (x-y) + \frac{1}{4}$.

24. $16x^8 - 81y^4$ by $27y^3 + 18x^2y^2 + 8x^6 + 12x^4y$.

25. $4x^4 - 10x^2 + 6$ by $x + 1$.

26. $4a^4 - 5a^2b^2 + b^4$ by $2a - b$.

27. $a^6 - b^6 + a^4 + b^4 + a^2b^2$ by $a^2 - b^2 + 1$.

28. $x^6 - y^6 - x^4 - y^4 - x^2y^2$ by $x^2 - y^2 - 1$.

29. $81a^{12} - 16b^8$ by $12a^3b^4 - 8b^6 - 18a^6b^2 + 27a^9$.

30. $1 + 3x$ by $1 + x$ to four terms of quotient.

31. $1 - 2a$ by $1 - a$ to four terms of quotient.

32. $4 + a$ by $2 - a$ to four terms.

33. $9 - x$ by $3 + x$ to four terms.

34. If a boy can do a piece of work in x minutes, how many hours would it take him to perform 12 times as much work?

35. A man has x dollars, y acres of land worth m dollars an acre, and c houses each worth b dollars. What is my share if I am one of n heirs?

36. A storekeeper mixed m pounds of coffee worth a cents a pound with p pounds worth b cents a pound. How much is the mixture worth per pound?

37. If John is y years old, how old was he 11 years ago?

EVOLUTION.

20. ILLUS. $\sqrt{a}$, $\sqrt[3]{x^2y}$, $\sqrt[4]{x-y}$, $\sqrt{16}$, $\sqrt[3]{5}$, $\sqrt[5]{6a^2bc}$.

The root of a number is indicated by the radical sign and index. When no index is expressed, *two* is understood.

Express:

1. The square root of x, $2ab$, $7x-3y^2$, a^2bc.
2. The fifth root of $3y$, $2m-n$, $4x^2yz^3$.
3. The cube root of 2, $x+y$, $17x^2y^4$, m.
4. The sixth root of az, $5m^2n-3xy+14-3ab^3c$.

What is the square root of a number? the fifth root? the fourth root? the cube root? the eleventh root?

ILLUS. 1. $(3a^2bc^3)^3 = ?$ Then $\sqrt[3]{27a^6b^3c^9} = ?$

ILLUS. 2. $\left.\begin{matrix}(+a)^4 = ? \\ (-a)^4 = ?\end{matrix}\right\}$ Hence $\sqrt[4]{+a^4} = ?$

$(+a)^3 = ?$ $\sqrt[3]{+a^3} = ?$

$(-a)^3 = ?$ $\sqrt[3]{-a^3} = ?$

To find the root of a monomial, find the required root of the coefficient, divide the exponent of each letter by the index of the root for the exponent of that letter in the root, give to even roots of plus numbers the plus-or-minus sign ($\pm$) , *to odd roots of plus numbers the plus sign, and to odd roots of minus numbers the minus sign.*

Exercise 27.

Simplify:

1. $\sqrt{16a^2b^6}$.
2. $\sqrt[4]{81x^4y^8}$.
3. $\sqrt[3]{-8x^6y^3}$.
4. $\sqrt[5]{-32a^{10}b^{15}}$.
5. $\sqrt[5]{243a^5b^{10}}$.

6. $\sqrt[3]{27x^3y^9}$.

7. $\sqrt[4]{16x^8y^4}$.

8. $\sqrt{9x^8y^6}$.

9. $\sqrt{\frac{4}{9}m^6y^4}$.

10. $\sqrt[3]{\frac{8}{27}a^9b^6}$.

11. $\sqrt[3]{-\frac{27}{64}x^9y^{12}}$.

12. $\sqrt[5]{-\frac{32}{243}a^5b^{15}}$.

13. $\sqrt[6]{x^{12}(a-b)^6}$.

14. $\sqrt[3]{a^9(x^2+y^2)^3}$.

15. $\sqrt{4a^2b^6(x^2-y)^4}$.

16. $\sqrt{16x^4y^2(m^3+y)^6}$.

17. $\sqrt{\frac{1}{9}a^4b^6} - \sqrt[3]{\frac{1}{8}a^6b^9} - \sqrt[5]{\frac{32}{243}a^{10}b^{15}} + \sqrt[3]{a^6b^9}$.

18. $\sqrt[3]{\frac{1}{8}x^6y^3} + \sqrt[5]{-\frac{1}{32}x^{10}y^5} - \sqrt[3]{-x^6y^3} - \sqrt{\frac{1}{4}x^4y^2}$.

19. Multiply $\sqrt{25a^4b^2c^2}$ by $-\sqrt[3]{-8a^3b^6c^9}$.

20. Divide $\sqrt{144x^4y^4}$ by $\sqrt[5]{243x^{10}y^5}$.

21. Multiply $-\sqrt[3]{-125x^3y^6z^6}$ by $\sqrt{9x^4y^2z^6}$.

22. Divide $\sqrt{100a^6b^{12}}$ by $\sqrt[5]{32a^{15}b^{25}}$.

23. From two cities a miles apart two trains start toward each other, the one going x miles an hour, and the other y miles an hour. How long before they will meet? How far will each train have gone?

24. What number is that whose double exceeds its half by 39?

25. Mr. A. is m years old, and 6 years ago he was one-half as old as Mr. B. How old was Mr. B. then? How old is Mr. B. now?

21. $(a+b)^2 = a^2 + 2ab + b^2 = a^2 + (2a+b)b.$

ILLUS. 1. Find the square root of $9x^2 - 12xy + 4y^2$.

$$\begin{array}{rrr|l}
 & & 9x^2 - 12xy + 4y^2 & 3x - 2y \\
a^2 = & & 9x^2 & \\ \cline{3-3}
2a+b = & 6x \quad -2y & \multicolumn{1}{|l}{-12xy + 4y^2} & \\
(2a+b)b = & & \multicolumn{1}{|l}{-12xy + 4y^2} & \\ \cline{3-3}
\end{array}$$

ILLUS. 2. Find the square root of $x^6 - 6x^3 - 4x + 1 + 6x^2 - 2x^5 + 5x^4$.

$$\begin{array}{rl}
 & x^6 \quad -2x^5 + 5x^4 - 6x^3 + 6x^2 - 4x + 1 \;\big|\; x^3 - x^2 + 2x - 1 \\
 & x^6 \\
 & 2x^3 \quad -x^2 \;\big|\; -2x^5 + 5x^4 - 6x^3 + 6x^2 - 4x + 1 \\
 & \qquad\qquad -2x^5 + x^4 \\
2(x^3 - x^2) + 2x = & 2x^3 \quad -x^2 \quad +2x \;\big|\; 4x^4 - 6x^3 + 6x^2 - 4x + 1 \\
 & \qquad\qquad\qquad 4x^4 - 4x^3 + 4x^2 \\
2(x^3 - x^2 + 2x) + (-1) = & 2x^3 \quad -2x^2 \quad +4x \quad -1 \;\big|\; -2x^3 + 2x^2 - 4x + 1 \\
 & \qquad\qquad\qquad\qquad -2x^3 + 2x^2 - 4x + 1
\end{array}$$

To find the square root of a polynomial, arrange the terms with reference to the powers of some number; take the square root of the first term of the polynomial for the first term of the root, and subtract its square from the polynomial; divide the first term of the remainder by twice the root found for the next term of the root, and add the quotient to the trial divisor; multiply the complete divisor by the second term of the root, and subtract the product from the remainder. If there is still a remainder, consider the root already found as one term, and proceed as before.

Exercise 28.

Find the square root of each of the following:

1. $4x^2 - 12xy + 9y^2$.
2. $x^4 + 10x^3y^3 + 25x^2y^6$.
3. $16a^2b^2c^4 - 56abc^2xy^2z + 49x^2y^4z^2$.
4. $\frac{1}{4}x^2 - xy^2z + y^4z^2$.
5. $a^2b^6 + \frac{2}{3}ab^3c^4 + \frac{1}{9}c^8$.
6. $x^4 - 4x^3 + 2x^2 + 4x + 1$.
7. $x^4 + 6x^3 + 17x^2 + 24x + 16$.
8. $4x^4 + 9x^2 + 4 - 4x - 4x^3$.
9. $6x^3 - 5x^2 + 1 - 2x + 9x^4$.
10. $x^6 + 2x^5 - x^4 + 3x^2 - 2x + 1$.

11. $6x^4 - 4x^3 + 4x^5 - 15x^2 - 8x + x^6 + 16$.

12. $7x^2 - 6x - 11x^4 + 10x^3 - 4x^5 + 1 + 4x^6$.

13. A is x years old. If his age is as much above 50 as B's age is below 40, what is B's age?

14. If x represents the first digit, and y the second digit, of a number, what will represent the number?

22. $(a+b)^3 = a^3 + 3a^2b + 3ab^2 + b^3 = a^3 + (3a^2 + 3ab + b^2)b$

ILLUS. 1. Find the cube root of $8m^6 + 12m^4n^3 + 6m^2n^6 + n^9$.

$$\begin{array}{rrl|l}
 & & 8m^6+12m^4n^3+6m^2n^6+n^9 & 2m^2+n^3 \\
a^3= & & 8m^6 & \\
\hline
3a^2+3ab+b^2= & 12m^4+6m^2n^3 & +n^6 \quad 12m^4n^3+6m^2n^6+n^9 & \\
(3a^2+3ab+b^2)b= & & \qquad\;\; 12m^4n^3+6m^2n^6+n^9 & \\
\hline
\end{array}$$

ILLUS. 2. Find the cube root of $66x^2 + 33x^4 + 8 - 36x + x^6 - 63x^3 - 9x^5$.

$$\begin{array}{rrl|l}
 & & x^6-9x^5+33x^4-63x^3+66x^2-36x+8 & x^2-3x+2 \\
 & & x^6 & \\
\hline
 & 3x^4-9x^3+9x^2 & -9x^5+33x^4-63x^3+66x^2-36x+8 & \\
 & & -9x^5+27x^4-27x^3 & \\
\hline
3(x^2-3x)^2= & 3x^4-18x^3+27x^2 & 6x^4-36x^3+66x^2-36x+8 & \\
3(x^2-3x)^2\times 2= & 6x^2-18x & & \\
2^2= & +4 & & \\
\hline
 & 3x^4-18x^3+33x^2-18x+4 & 6x^4-36x^3+66x^2-36x+8 & \\
\hline
\end{array}$$

To find the cube root of a polynomial, arrange the terms with reference to the powers of some number; take the cube root of the first term for the first term of the root, and subtract its cube from the polynomial; take three times the square of the root already found for a trial divisor, divide the first term of the remainder by it, and write the quotient for the next term of the root; add to the trial divisor three times the product of the first term by the second and the square of the second; multiply the complete divisor by the second term of the root, and subtract the product from the remainder. If there are other terms remaining, consider the root already found as one term, and proceed as before.

Exercise 29

Find the cube root of each of the following:

1. $27x^3 - 27x^2y + 9xy^2 - y^3$.
2. $15x^2 - 1 - 75x^4 + 125x^6$.
3. $144a^2b^2 + 27b^6 + 108ab^4 + 64a^3$.

4. $x^6 - 8y^6 + 12x^2y^4 - 6x^4y^2$.

5. $1 + 9x + 27x^2 + 27x3$.

6. $1 - 21m - 343m^3 + 147m^2$.

7. $3x^2 + 64x^6 - 24x^4 - \frac{1}{8}$.

8. $27x^9 + \frac{1}{27} + x^3 + 9x^6$.

9. $8a^6 + 18a^4 + 9a^2 - 12a^5 - 13a^3 - 3a + 1$.

10. $x^9 - 7x^6 + x^3 - 3x^4 - 3x^8 + 6x^7 + 6x^5$.

11. $5x^3 - 3x - 3x^5 - 1 + x^6$.

12. $\frac{1}{8}a^6 + \frac{3}{2}a^5 + 5\frac{1}{4}a^4 + 2a^3 - 10\frac{1}{2}a^2 + 6a - 1$.

13. A board is $8x$ inches long and $2x$ inches wide. What is the length of a square board having the same area?

14. If $3x$ represents the edge of a cubical box, what represents the cubical contents of the box?

15. If a cubical cistern contains $64y^3$ cubic feet, how long is one edge?

16. A man travels north a miles, and then south b miles. How far is he from the starting-point? How far has he traveled?

Exercise 30.

Find the indicated roots:

1. $\sqrt{2025}$.

2. $\sqrt{9409}$.

3. $\sqrt{20449}$.

4. $\sqrt{904401}$.

5. $\sqrt{70.56}$.

6. $\sqrt{.9025}$.

7. $\sqrt{94864}$.

8. $\sqrt{.00000784}$

9. $\sqrt[3]{59.319}$.

10. $\sqrt[3]{389017}$.

11. $\sqrt[3]{241804.367}$.

12. $\sqrt{7039.21}$.

13. $\sqrt[3]{35.287552}$.

14. $\sqrt{2550.25}$.

15. $\sqrt{34.78312}$ to three decimal places.

16. $\sqrt{7}$ to three decimal places.

17. $\sqrt[3]{.1255}$ to three decimal places.

18. A merchant bought a bale of cloth containing just as many pieces as there were yards in each piece. The whole number of yards was 1089. What was the number of pieces?

19. A regiment, consisting of 5476 men, is to be formed into a solid square. How many men must be placed in each rank?

20. What is the depth of a cubical cistern which contains 5000 gallons of water? (1 gallon = 231 cubic inches.)

21. A farmer plants an orchard containing 8464 trees, and has as many rows of trees as there are trees in each row. What is the number of trees in each row?

FACTORS AND MULTIPLES

FACTORING.

23. When we divide a number into two numbers, which multiplied together will give a product equal to the given number, we have found the factors of that number. This process is called **factoring**.

Name two factors of 48, 27, 18, 35, 49, 72.

Name three factors of 24, 100, 75, 64, 72, 40.

24. CASE I. To factor a polynomial which has a factor common to all its terms.

ILLUS. Factor $2ab + 6ac + 4ad$.

$$2a \,\underline{\big|\; 2ab + 6ac + 4ad \qquad\qquad}$$
$$b + 3c + 2d$$
$$\therefore 2ab + 6ac + 4ad = 2a\,(b + 3c + 2d).$$

Divide the polynomial by the largest factor common to the terms. The quotient and divisor are the factors of the polynomial.

Exercise 31.

Factor:

1. $5a^2 - 25$.
2. $16 + 64xy$.
3. $2a - 2a^2$.
4. $15a^2 - 225a^4$.
5. $x^3 - x^2$.
6. $3a^2 + a^5$.
7. $a^2 - ab^2$.

8. $a^2 + ab$.

9. $6a^3 + 2a^4 + 4a^5$.

10. $7x - 7x^3 + 14x^4$.

11. $3x^3 - x^2 + x$.

12. $a^3 - a^2y + ay^2$.

13. $3a(x + y) + 5mb(x + y) - 9d^2x(x + y)$.

14. $4(a - b) - 15xy(a - b) + (a - b) - 5a^2b(a - b)$.

15. $4x^3y - 12ax^2 - 8xy^3$.

16. $6ax^3y^5 - 4ax^2y^6 + 2axy^7 - 2a^2xy^9$.

17. $51x^5y - 34x^4y^2 + 17x^2y^4$.

18. $6a^2b^2 - 3a^3b^3c - 9ab^3c + 3abc^2$.

19. $3ax^7 - 24ax + 9ax^5 - 3ax^4 - 9ax^6$.

20. $27a^8b^2c^3 - 81a^7b^3c^3 + 81a^6b^4c^3 - 27a^5b^5c^3 - 27a^5b^2c^6$.

21. A lady bought a ribbon for m cents, some tape for d cents, and some thread for c cents, for which she paid x cents on account. How much remains due?

22. Julia has the same number of beads in each hand. If she should change two from her left hand to her right hand, the right hand would contain twice as many as the left. How many beads has she?

Sometimes a polynomial in the form given has no factor common to all its terms, but has factors common to several terms. It may be possible then to group the terms in parentheses so that there will be a binomial or trinomial factor common to all the terms of the polynomial in its new form.

ILLUS. 1. Factor $2am + 2ax + bm + bx$.

$$2am + 2ax + bm + bx = 2a(m + x) + b(m + x).$$

$$m + x \;\underline{\big|\; 2a(m + x) \quad +b(m + x)}$$
$$2a \qquad\qquad +b$$

$$\therefore 2am + 2ax + bm + bx = (m + x)(2a + b).$$

ILLUS. 2. Factor $a^8 + a^6 - a^5 - a^3 + a^2 + 1$.

$$a^8 + a^6 - a^5 - a^3 + a^2 + 1 = a^6(a^2 + 1) - a^3(a^2 + 1) + (a^2 + 1).$$

$$a^2 + 1 \;\underline{\big|\; a^6(a^2 + 1) \quad -a^3(a^2 + 1) \quad +(a^2 + 1)}$$
$$a^6 \qquad\qquad -a^3 \qquad\qquad +1$$

$$\therefore a^8 + a^6 - a^5 - a^3 + a^2 + 1 = (a^2 + 1)(a^6 - a^3 + 1).$$

Exercise 32.

Factor:

1. $ax + ay + bx + by$.
2. $x^2 + ax + bx + ab$.
3. $ax^2 + ay^2 - bx^2 - by^2$.
4. $x^2 - ax + 5x - 5a$.
5. $ax - bx + ab - x^2$.
6. $x^2 + mxy - 4xy - 4my^2$.
7. $2x^4 - x^3 + 4x - 2$.
8. $mx - ma - nx + na$.
9. $x^3 + x^2 + x + 1$.
10. $y^3 - y^2 + y - 1$.
11. $x^5 + x^4 - x^3 - x^2 + x + 1$.
12. $a^2x + abx + ac + aby + b^2y + bc$.
13. $ax - bx + by + cy - cx - ay$.
14. $3ax + 3ay - 2bx - 2by$.
15. $2ax - 3by + cy - 2ay + 3bx - cx$.
16. $6amx + 3amy - 6anx - 3any$.
17. A man had 250 acres of land and 30 houses. After trading x of his houses for y acres of land, how many has he of each?
18. What is the number that will become four times as large by adding 36 to it?
19. The fifth and seventh of a number are together equal to 24. What is the number?

25. CASE II. To factor the difference of the squares of two numbers.

ILLUS. 1. $a^2 - b^2 = (a + b)(a - b)$.
ILLUS. 2. $9x^2y^4 - 49a^4b^{12} = (3xy^2 + 7a^2b^6)(3xy^2 - 7a^2b^6)$.
ILLUS. 3.

$$\begin{aligned} x^8 - y^8 &= (x^4 + y^4)(x^4 - y^4) = (x^4 + y^4)(x^2 + y^2)(x^2 - y^2) \\ &= (x^4 + y^4)(x^2 + y^2)(x + y)(x - y). \end{aligned}$$

Write two factors, of which one is the sum and the other the difference of the square roots of the terms.

Exercise 33.

Factor:

1. $x^2 - y^2$.
2. $m^2 - n^2$.
3. $a^2b^4 - c^2d^2$.
4. $m^2p^4 - x^6y^4$.
5. $a^6b^2x^4 - m^4c^8y^{10}$.
6. $x^2y^4z^4 - c^2d^2m^4$.
7. $x^4y^2 - a^6y^4$.
8. $g^6c^6 - x^6z^8$.
9. $4a^2 - 9x^2$.
10. $16m^2 - 9n^2$.
11. $81x^2y^4 - 25b^2d^2$.
12. $729m^4c^2x^{10} - 10,000y^4$.
13. $121m^2 - 64x^2$.
14. $x^4 - y^4$.
15. $m^8 - a^8$.
16. $a^4b^8 - l$.
17. $x^16 - b^16$.
18. $16a^4 - 1$.
19. $a^4 - ax^2$.
20. $5b^4 - 5a^2b^2$.
21. $ax^2 - ay^2 - bx^2 + by^2$.
22. $5ax - 5a^3x + 5ay - 5a^3y$.
23. $m^2 - y^2 - am + ay$.
24. $a^2 - x^2 - a - x$.
25. By how much does x exceed $3y$?
26. Eleven years ago C was three times as old as D whose age was x years. What is C's present age ?

26. CASE III. To factor the sum of the cubes of two numbers.
ILLUS. 1. Divide $a^3 + b^2$ by $a + b$.
ILLUS. 2. Divide $m^3 + n^3y^3$ by $m + ny$.
ILLUS. 3. Divide $8a^6 + b^3c^9$ by $2a^2 + bc^3$.
Notice in each case above:

1. That the divisor is the sum of the cube roots of the terms of the dividend.

2. That the quotient is the square of the first term of the divisor, minus the product of the first term by the second, plus the square of the second.

Write two factors, one of which is the sum of the cube roots of the terms, and the other the quotient obtained by dividing the original number by the first factor.

Exercise 34

Factor:

1. $x^5 + y^5$
2. $c^3 + d^3$
3. $a^3 + b^3c^3$
4. $a^3x^3 + y^3$
5. $8a^5b^3c^6 + m^6$
6. $x^6y^3 + 216a^3$
7. $a^6 + b^6$
8. $64x^6 + y^6$
9. $x^3 + 8$
10. $27 + a^3b^6$
11. $y^3 + 1$
12. $1 + b^3c^3$
13. $\frac{1}{8}a^6b^3 + c^0$
14. $\frac{1}{27}x^3 + 1$
15. $(m + n)^3 + 8$
16. $1 + (x - y)^3$
17. $2a^2x^3y^6 + 2a^8b^9$

18. $mx + my - nx - ny$

19. $a^3x + b^3x - a^3y - b^3y$

20. $a^6 - b^6$

21. $729x^6 - 64y^6$

22. $1 - x^8$

23. A had d dollars, but, after giving \$26 to B, he had one-third as many as B. How many has B? How many had B at first?

24. How many units in y tens?

25. If the sum of two numbers is x, and one of the numbers is 8, what is the other number?

26. What does a^3 mean? What does $3a$ stand for? What is the product of x^4 and 0?

27. CASE IV. To factor the difference of the cubes of two numbers.
ILLUS. I. Divide $a^3 - b^3$ by $a - b$.
ILLUS. 2. Divide $27a^6b^9 - c^3d^12$ by $3a^2b^3 - cd^4$.
Notice in each case above:

1. That the divisor is the difference of the cube roots of the terms of the dividend.

2. That the quotient is the square of the first term of the divisor, plus the product of the first by the second, plus the square of the second.

Write two factors, one of which is the difference of the cube roots of the terms, and the other the quotient obtained by dividing the original number by the first factor.

Exercise 35.

Factor:

1. $x^3 - a^3$

2. $c^3 - b^3$

3. $a^3 - x^3y^3$.

4. $m^3n^3 - c^3$.

5. $27m^3 - 8x^3$.

6. $8x^3 - 64y^3$

7. $64a^3x^6b^3 - 125m^9c^3y^6$.

8. $27b^3c^6y^3 - 216a^9m^6x^6$.

9. $8x^9y^3 - 125$.

10. $27 - 64m^3x^6y^3$.

11. $a^3 - b^6$.

12. $m^6 - x^3$.

13. $x^3 - 1$.

14. $1 - y^3$.

15. $\frac{1}{27}x^3y^6 - b^9$.

16. $8 - \frac{1}{64}m^6n^3$.

17. $1 - (a+b)^3$.

18. $x^3y^3 - (x - y^2)^3$.

19. $x^7 - xy^3$.

20. $ab^3 - ac^3 + mb^3 - mc^3$.

21. $x^6 - y^6$ into four factors.

22. $x^6 - x^5 + x^3 - x^2 - x + 1$.

23. $a^2 - b^2 + a^3 - b^3$.

24. $mx^3 + my^3 - x - y$.

25. How many hours will it take x men to dig 75 bushels of potatoes if each man digs y bushels an hour?

26. If there are x tens, y units, and z hundreds in a number, what will represent the whole number of units?

28. CASE V. To factor trinomials which are perfect squares.

Square $c+b, c-b, x^2-y^2, 3mn^3+y^2, 2a^2bc-3x^2yz^3$. How are the first and last terms of these trinomial squares formed? How is the middle term formed?

When is a trinomial a square?

Name those of the following trinomials which are squares:

1. $m^2 - 2mp + p^2$.

2. $x^2 + 2xy - y^2$.

3. $4x^2 - 4xy + y^2$.

4. $x^4 + 6x^2y + 9y^2$.

5. $a^4 - 18a^2 + 9$.

6. $9b^4 + 12d^2 + 4$.

7. $16y^4 - 8y^2 + 1$.

8. $25c^8d^6 + 20c^4d^3x + 4x^2$.

ILLUS. 1. $a^2 + 2ab + b^2 = (a + b)(a + b) = (a + b)^2$.
ILLUS. 2. $a - 2ab + b = (a - b)(a - b) = (a - b)^2$.
ILLUS. 3. $9a^2 - 12ab + 4b^2 = (3a - 2b)^2$.

Write two binomial factors, each of which consists of the square roots of the squares connected by the sign of the middle term.

Exercise 36.

Factor:

1. $a^2 + 2ax + x^2$.
2. $c^2 - 2cd + d^2$.
3. $4a^2 + 4ay + y^2$.
4. $a^2 + 4ab + 4b^2$.
5. $x^2 - 6cx + 9c^2$.
6. $16x^2 - 8xy + y^2$.
7. $a^2 + 2a + 1$.
8. $9 - 6x + x^2$.
9. $x^2 - 10x + 25$.
10. $4y^2 - 12y + 9$.
11. $9x^2 + 24x + 16$.
12. $81a^4 - 18a^2 + 1$.
13. $9c^2 + 66cd + 121d^2$.
14. $4y^2 - 36y + 81$.
15. $x^4 - 6x^2y + 9y^2$.
16. $9 - 12x^2 + 4x^4$.
17. $16x^2y^4 - 24a^3xy^2 + 9a^6$.

18. $25b^2 + 30bc^2y + 9c^4y^2$.

19. $49a^2 + 28ax^2y + 4x^4y^2$.

20. $\frac{1}{9}x^4 - \frac{2}{3}x^2y^2 + 4y^4$.

21. $\frac{1}{4}a^2 + 2ab + 4b^2$.

22. $\frac{4}{9}x^6y^2 - \frac{4}{3}x^3yz^4 + z^8$.

23. $x^9 - 4x^6y^4 + 4x^3y^8$.

24. $18a^2y + 24ay^3 + 8y^5$.

25. $3a^3x^5 - 30a^2bx^4 + 75ab^2x^3$.

26. $(x+y)^2 - 2a^2(x+y) + a^4$.

27. $(m^2 - n^2)^2 - 2(m^4 - n^4) + (m^2 + n^2)^2$.

28. $a^2 + 2ab + b^2 + 6a + 6b$.

29. $x^2 + y^2 - 3x - 2xy + 3y$.

30. $x^6 + y^6 - 2x^3y^3$.

What must be added to the following to make them perfect squares?

31. $a^2 + 2xy$.

32. $m^6 + 6m^3y$.

33. $c^2 + d^2$.

34. $(x-y)^4 + 2(x-y)^2$.

35. $(c-d)^2 - 6(c-d)$.

36. $9x^4y^2 - 12x^2y^3$.

37. $30xy^4 + 9x^2y^6$.

38. $25a^2b^2 + 36b^4c^2$.

39. $49a^2b^2c^2 + 25a^2b^4d^2$.

40. $a^4 - 22a^2 + 9$ (two numbers).

41. $64a^2 - 177ay + 121y^2$.

42. $a^4 - 10a^2b^2 + 9b^4$.

43. $x^4 + x^2 + 1$.

44. $a^2 + a + 1$.

45. A stream flows at the rate of a miles an hour, and a man can row in still water b miles an hour. How far can the man row up the stream in an hour? In 6 hours? How far down the stream in an hour? In 3 hours?

46. A cistern can he filled by two pipes in 3 hours and 5 hours respectively. What part of the cistern will be filled by both pipes running together for one hour?

47. Nine years ago Henry was three times as old as Julius. If Henry is b years old, how old was Julius then? How old is Julius now?

29. CASE VI. To factor trinomials in the form $x^2 \pm cx \pm d$.
This is the reverse of the case under Multiplication given in Art. 14.
ILLUS. 1. $x^2 + 14x + 45 = (x + 9)(x + 5)$.
ILLUS. 2. $x^2 - 6x + 5 = (x - 5)(x - 1)$.
ILLUS. 3. $x^2 + 2x - 3 = (x + 3)(x - 1)$.
ILLUS. 4. $x^2 - 8x - 20 = (x - 10)(x + 2)$.

Write two binomial factors, the first term of each being the square root of the first term of the given trinomial, and for the second terms of the factors find two numbers whose algebraic sum is the coefficient of the second term and whose product is the last term.

Exercise 37.

Factor:

1. $a^2 + 3a + 2$.
2. $x^2 + 9x + 18$.
3. $x^2 - 5x + 6$.
4. $a^2 - 7a + 10$.
5. $y^2 - 10y + 16$.
6. $c^2 - c - 6$.
7. $x^2 + 4x - 5$.
8. $x^2 + 5x - 6$.
9. $y^2 + 8y - 65$.
10. $a^2 - 4a - 77$.
11. $x^2 - 2x - 63$.
12. $a^2 + 10a - 75$.
13. $a^2 - 24a + 143$.

14. $x^6 - 4x^3 - 117$.

15. $x^6 + 4x^3 - 77$.

16. $30 + 11x + x^2$.

17. $21 + 10a + a^2$.

18. $35 - 12x + x^2$.

19. $36 - 13x + x^2$.

20. $c^2 + 2cd - 3d^2$.

21. $a^2 + 8ax + 15x^2$.

22. $x^2 - xy - 20y^2$.

23. $x^4 + x^2y - 12y^2$.

24. $x^4 - 14x^2y^2 + 45y^4$.

25. $x^5 - 23x^4 + 132x^3$.

26. $a^6 - 12a^5 + 35a^4$.

27. $3ax^4 - 39ax^2 + 108a$.

28. $3a^3 - 12a^2b + 12ab^2$.

29. $c^5d^3 - c^2 - a^2c^3d^3 + a^2$.

30. $ax^2 + bx^2 - 5bx - 5ax + 6b + 6a$.

31. A field can be mowed by two men in a hours and b hours respectively. What part of the field can be mowed by both men working together for one hour?

32. In how many days can two men do as much as x men in 7 days?

Exercise 38. (Review.)

1. Divide $50a + 9a^4 + 24 - 67a^2$ by $a + a^2 - 6$.

2. Find the square root of

$$12y^5 - 14y^3 + 1 - 8y^4 + 4y + 9y^6.$$

3. Expand $(x + y)(x - y)(x^2 + y^2)$.

4. What must be subtracted from $a^3 - 5a^2 + 27a - 1$ to produce $a + 1$?

5. Expand $\left(x^2y - 4z^3a^4\right)^3$.

Factor:

6. $x^2 - 11x + 10$.

7. $(a+b)^2 - (c+d)^2$.

8. $6x^3 + 4x^2 - 9x - 6$.

9. $9x^8 - 66x^6 + 121x^4$.

10. $8c^6 - d^9$.

11. $1 + 64x^3$.

12. $a^6 - 1$.

13. $x^3 + 2x^2 - x - 2$.

14. $x^5 - y^5$.

15. $27 + 12x + x^2$.

16. Find the cube root of $96m - 64 - 40m^3 + m^6 + 6m^5$.

17. Simplify $(m+2n)^2 - (2m-n)^2$.

18. Simplify $(5+7x)(5-7x) - (3+2x)^2 + (x-9)(x-4)$.

19. Simplify $(y+x)(y^2 - xy + x^2) - (y-x)(y^2 + yx + x^2)$.

20. Find three consecutive numbers whose sum is 57.

21. What number, being increased by three-fifths of itself, will equal twice itself diminished by 24?

22. Find the value of $(4a+5b)(3a+4b) - a^2b + b^3c^2 - c^3$ when $a = 0$, $b = 1$, and $c = 2$.

GREATEST COMMON FACTOR.

30. What are the factors of $9a^4b^2 + 9a^3b^3$? Of $3a^4b - 3a^2b^3$? Which are factors of each of them? What is the largest number that is a factor of each of them? This number is called their *Greatest Common Factor.* What factors of the numbers does it contain?

ILLUS. Find the G.C.F. of

$$3ac + 3bc \text{ and } 6a^2x + 12abx + 6b^2x.$$

$$\begin{aligned} 3ac + 3bc &= 3c(a+b) \\ 6a^2x + 12abx + 6b^2x &= 6x(a+b)(a+b) \\ G.C.F. &= 3(a+b) = 3a + 3b \end{aligned}$$

To find the G.C.F. of two or more numbers, find the prime factors of each of the numbers and take the product of the common factors.

Exercise 39.

Find the G.C.F. of each of the following:

1. $3a^4b^3 + 6a^2b^5$ and $9a^3b^2 + 18ab^3$.
2. $5x^5y - 15x^2y^2$ and $15x^3y^3 - 45xy^5$.
3. $2x^5y^4 + 2x^2y^7$ and $6x^3y^3 - 6xy^5$.
4. $3a^6b - 3a^3b^4$ and $12a^4b^4 - 12a^2b^6$.
5. $mx - ma - nx + na$ and $m^3 - n^3$.
6. $81x^8 - 16$ and $81x^8 - 72x^4 + 16$.
7. $x^2 - 20 - x$, $3x^2 - 24x + 45$, and $x^2 - 5x$.
8. $x^2 + x - 6$, $x^2 - 15 - 2x$, and $3x^2 - 27$.
9. $a^4 - 16$, $a2 - a - 6$, and $(a^2 - 4)^2$.
10. $y^3 - y$, $y^3 + 9y^2 - 10y$, and $y^4 - y$.
11. $x^2 - y^2$, $xy - y^2 + xz - yz$, and $x^3 - x^2y + xy^2 - y^3$.
12. $3ac^5d^3 - 3ac^2 - 3a^3c^3d^3 + 3a3$ and $9a^2c^4 - 9a^6$.
13. $64x^{11} - 8x^2y^6$ and $12x^8 + 3x^2y^4 - 12x^5y^2$.
14. A merchant mixes a pounds of tea worth x cents a pound with b pounds worth y cents a pound. How much is the mixture worth per pound?
15. If a man bought a horse for x dollars and sold him so as to gain 5%, what will represent the number of dollars he gained?
16. The difference between two numbers is 6, and if 4 be added to the greater, the result will be three times the smaller. What are the numbers?

    Of how many terms does the expression $x^3 - 4x^2y + y^3$ consist? How many factors has each of the terms? What is the value of a number, one of whose factors is zero?

LEAST COMMON MULTIPLE.

31. ILLUS. 1. $12a^2b^3$ is the least common multiple of $3a^2b$ and $4ab^3$. How many of the factors of $3a^2b$ are found in the L.C.M.? How many of the factors of $4ab^3$?

ILLUS. 2. Find the L.C.M. of $9ac + 9bc$, $3a^2x - 3b^2x$, and $ax^2 - bx^2$.

$$\begin{aligned} 9ac + 9bc &= 9c(a+b) \\ 3a^2x - 3b^2x &= 3x(a+b)(a-b) \\ ax^2 - bx^2 &= x^2(a-b) \\ \hline \text{L.C.M.} &= 9cx^2(a+b)(a-b) \end{aligned}$$

To find the L.C.M. of two or more numbers, find the prime factors of each number, take the product of the different factors, using each the greatest number of times it is found in any of the numbers.

Exercise 40

Find the L.C.M. of each of the following:

1. $a^2 - 4$ and $a^2 + 3a - 10$.
2. $x^3 + 1$ and $x^2 + 2x + 1$.
3. $x^2 - 2x - 15$ and $x^2 - 9$.
4. $x^4 - 4x^2 + 3$ and $x^6 - 1$.
5. $x^2 - 1$, $x^2 - 4x + 3$, and $2x^2 - 2x - 12$.
6. $a^3 + 1 + 3a + 3a^2$ and $am - 2 - 2a + m$.
7. $a^2 - 4$, $a^2 + 3a - 10$, $a^2 - 25$, $a^2 - 9$, $a^2 - 8a + 15$, and $a^2 + 5a + 6$.
8. $x^3 - 1 - 3x^2 + 3x$ and $xy - 3 - y + 3x$.
9. $x^2 - 1$, $x^2 - 9$, $x^2 - 2x - 3$, $x^2 - 16$, $x^2 - x - 12$, $x^2 + 5x + 4$.
10. $x^6 + x^3$, $2x^4 - 2x^2$, and $x^2 + x$.
11. $a^4 + 2a^2 + 1$, $1 - 2a^2 + a^4$, and $1 - a^4$.
12. $a^2z - x^2z$, $3ax - 3x^2$, and $2ax + 2a^2$.
13. $am + an - 3m - 3n$, $m^2 - n^2$, and $a^2 - 10a + 21$.
14. $3b - 3b^2$, $1 - b^3$, and $2x - 2b^2x$.
15. $a^2 - x^2 - a - x$, $5a^2b - 10abx + 5bx^2$, and $a^2b - abx - ab$.
16. The thermometer now indicates c degrees above zero, but yesterday it indicated y degrees below zero. How much warmer is it to-day than yesterday?
17. A certain county extends from b degrees north latitude to y degrees north latitude. What is the extent of the county from north to south?
18. If A can build a wall in x days, what part of the wall will he build in two days?
19. How many times can $x^3 + 12$ be subtracted from $x^6 + 24x^3 + 144$?
20. Divide \$2142 between two men so that one shall receive six times as much as the other.

Exercise 41.[4]

1. Reduce to lowest terms:

   $\frac{3}{6}$, $\frac{6}{9}$, $\frac{4}{10}$, $\frac{12}{14}$, $\frac{2}{16}$, $\frac{9}{36}$, $\frac{8}{22}$, $\frac{8}{20}$, $\frac{7}{8}$, $\frac{9}{30}$, $\frac{25}{150}$, $\frac{490}{560}$, $\frac{75}{325}$.

2. Change:

   a. $\frac{1}{4}$ to 8*ths*.

   b. $\frac{5}{6}$ to 12*ths*.

   c. $\frac{7}{8}$ to 32*ds*.

   d. $\frac{3}{5}$ to 25*ths*.

   e. $\frac{2}{3}$ to 21*sts*.

   f. $\frac{9}{10}$ to 50*ths*.

   g. $\frac{3}{7}$ to 28*ths*.

   h. $\frac{5}{9}$ to 36*ths*.

   i. $\frac{6}{13}$ to 39*ths*.

3. How many 15ths in $\frac{3}{5}$, $\frac{2}{3}$, $\frac{4}{5}$, 3, $1\frac{2}{5}$, $2\frac{2}{3}$?

4. How many 12ths in $\frac{1}{6}$, $\frac{3}{4}$, $\frac{5}{6}$, 4, 9, $2\frac{1}{3}$, $7\frac{3}{6}$?

5. Change to equivalent fractions:

   a. $2\frac{5}{6}$.

   b. $3\frac{3}{4}$.

   c. $12\frac{2}{3}$.

   d. $27\frac{1}{8}$.

   e. $9\frac{6}{7}$.

   f. $18\frac{2}{5}$.

6. Change to equivalent entire or mixed numbers:

   a. $\frac{12}{6}$.

   b. $\frac{15}{8}$.

   c. $\frac{17}{4}$.

   d. $\frac{84}{12}$.

   e. $\frac{57}{8}$.

   f. $\frac{61}{5}$.

   g. $\frac{125}{6}$.

   h. $\frac{97}{11}$.

   i. $\frac{225}{7}$.

[4]This exercise should be conducted orally, and if, at any point, the students do not readily recall the method, the examples of that class should be duplicated till the principle is clear.

7. Change to equivalent fractions having L. C. D.:
   a. $\frac{1}{2}, \frac{3}{4}, \frac{2}{3}$.
   b. $\frac{2}{3}, \frac{5}{8}, \frac{7}{12}$.
   c. $\frac{1}{4}, \frac{2}{5}, \frac{3}{10}$.
   d. $\frac{2}{3}, \frac{4}{5}, \frac{1}{6}$.
   e. $\frac{7}{8}, \frac{1}{5}, \frac{1}{2}$.
   f. $\frac{14}{15}, \frac{11}{20}, \frac{7}{9}, \frac{1}{5}$.
8. Add:
   a. $\frac{1}{2}$ and $\frac{1}{3}$.
   b. $\frac{1}{4}$ and $\frac{1}{5}$.
   c. $\frac{1}{6}$ and $\frac{1}{2}$.
   d. $\frac{2}{3}$ and $\frac{3}{4}$.
   e. $\frac{2}{5}$ and $\frac{1}{6}$.
   f. $\frac{3}{7}$ and $\frac{5}{6}$.
   g. $2\frac{1}{3}$ and $3\frac{1}{5}$.
   h. $4\frac{2}{5}$ and $11\frac{5}{6}$.
   i. $14\frac{3}{4}$ and $27\frac{4}{7}$.
9. Subtract:
   a. $\frac{1}{4}$ from $\frac{1}{2}$.
   b. $\frac{1}{7}$ from $\frac{1}{4}$.
   c. $\frac{1}{9}$ from $\frac{1}{6}$.
   d. $\frac{2}{5}$ from $\frac{7}{10}$.
   e. $\frac{3}{7}$ from $\frac{5}{6}$.
   f. $\frac{4}{9}$ from $\frac{1}{2}$.
   g. $2\frac{1}{5}$ from $5\frac{1}{2}$.
   h. $6\frac{3}{5}$ from $15\frac{3}{6}$.
   i. $27\frac{7}{8}$ from $29\frac{1}{3}$.
10. Find the product of:
   a. $\frac{2}{7}$ by 3.
   b. $\frac{3}{10}$ by 2.
   c. $\frac{3}{8}$ by 6.
   d. 5 by $\frac{2}{9}$.
   e. 9 by $\frac{7}{18}$.
   f. 4 by $\frac{5}{6}$.

g. $2\frac{3}{4}$ by 5.

h. $12\frac{3}{9}$ by 3.

i. 25 by $2\frac{2}{5}$.

j. $\frac{1}{2}$ by $\frac{1}{5}$.

k. $\frac{1}{3}$ by $\frac{4}{5}$.

l. $\frac{5}{9}$ by $\frac{3}{7}$.

m. $\frac{33}{54}$ by $\frac{12}{44}$.

n. $15\frac{2}{5}$ by $\frac{2}{3}$.

o. $24\frac{1}{4}$ by $\frac{5}{8}$.

p. $36\frac{2}{5}$ by $\frac{5}{9}$.

q. $2\frac{1}{3}$ by $5\frac{1}{2}$.

r. $3\frac{5}{6}$ by $4\frac{3}{5}$.

11. Divide:

a. $\frac{12}{17}$ by 3.

b. $\frac{10}{27}$ by 5.

c. $\frac{5}{7}$ by 4.

d. $\frac{3}{4}$ by 12.

e. $728\frac{14}{15}$ by 7.

f. $843\frac{1}{5}$ by 8.

g. $679\frac{1}{2}$ by 6.

h. $\frac{1}{4}$ by $\frac{1}{8}$.

i. $\frac{2}{3}$ by $\frac{2}{7}$.

j. $\frac{4}{9}$ by $\frac{3}{8}$.

k. 6 by $\frac{2}{3}$.

l. 9 by $\frac{5}{6}$.

m. $\frac{12}{25}$ by $\frac{9}{20}$.

n. $3\frac{1}{2}$ by $1\frac{3}{4}$.

o. $3\frac{3}{5}$ by $2\frac{2}{5}$.

p. 48 by $3\frac{1}{5}$.

q. 63 by $4\frac{2}{3}$.

r. $\frac{5}{6}$ by $\frac{3}{8}$.

12. Simplify:

a. $\frac{4}{5} + \frac{1}{2} - \frac{1}{3} = ?$

b. $\frac{\frac{3}{4}+\frac{2}{3}}{\frac{3}{4}-\frac{2}{3}} = ?$

c. $\frac{5}{6} - \frac{1}{4} + \frac{4}{5} = ?$

d. $\frac{2\frac{1}{3}}{4\frac{1}{5}} = ?$

13. 16 is $\frac{4}{7}$ of what number?

14. $\frac{3}{4}$ is what part of 7?

15. $\frac{2}{5}$ is what part of $\frac{5}{6}$?

16. What is $\frac{5}{8}$ of $\frac{4}{15}$?

17. If $\frac{2}{3}$ of a number is 20, what is $\frac{2}{5}$ of the number?

18. $\frac{2}{3}$ of 60 is $\frac{4}{9}$ of what number?

FRACTIONS.

32. In the previous exercise the different operations performed upon fractions in arithmetic have been reviewed. The principles and methods of operation are the same in algebra.

REDUCTION OF FRACTIONS.

33. ILLUS. 1. Reduce $\frac{5a^2b}{10ab^2}$ to lowest terms.

$$\frac{5a^2b \div 5ab}{10ab^2 \div 5ab} = \frac{a}{2b}$$

ILLUS. 2. Reduce $\frac{a^2bx-b^3x}{a^2bx-ab^2x}$ to lowest terms.

$$\frac{a^2bx - b^3x}{a^2bx - ab^2x} = \frac{bx(a^2 - b^2) \div bx(a - b)}{abx(a - b) \div bx(a - b)} = \frac{a + b}{a}$$

To reduce a fraction to its lowest terms, divide the terms of the fraction by their greatest common factor.

Exercise 42.

Reduce to lowest terms:

1. $\frac{15x^3y^2z}{40x^2y^2z^2}$.

2. $\frac{12x^5y^2z^3}{30xy^3z^3}$.

3. $\frac{x^2 - 7x + 12}{x^3 + x - 20}$.

4. $\frac{x^2 + 9x + 18}{x^2 - 2x - 15}$.

5. $\frac{a^6 + a^4}{a^4 - 1}$

6. $\dfrac{x^5 - x^2}{x^6 - 1}$

7. $\dfrac{mx - ny + nx - my}{ax - 2by + 2bx - ay}$

8. $\dfrac{ac - bd + ad - bc}{ax - 2by + 2ay - bx}$

9. $\dfrac{ac^2d - a^3d^3}{a^3c + a^4d}$

10. $\dfrac{a^2xy - x^3y^3}{ax^2 - x^3y}$

11. $\dfrac{a^4 - b^4}{(a^2 + 2ab + b^2)(a^2 + b^2)}$

12. $\dfrac{x^8 - y^8}{(x^4 + y^4)(x^4 - 2x^2y^2 + y^4)}$

13. $\dfrac{a^2x^2 - 16a^2}{ax^2 + 9ax + 20a}$

14. $\dfrac{a^4 - 14a^2 - 51}{a^4 - 2a^2 - 15}$

15. $\dfrac{3 + 4x + x^2}{6 + 5x + x^2}$

16. $\dfrac{a^2 - a^2b^2}{(a - ab)^2}$

17. At two-thirds of a cent apiece, what b apples cost?

18. James is x times as old as George. If James is a years old, how old is George?

34. ILLUS. 1. Change $\frac{ac-bc-d}{c}$ to an equivalent entire or mixed number.

$$\frac{ac - bc - d}{c} = a - b - \frac{d}{c}$$

To find an entire or mixed number equivalent to a given fraction, divide the numerator by the denominator.

ILLUS. 2. Change to equivalent fractions $b + \frac{a}{c}$, $b - \frac{a-x}{c}$.

$$b + \frac{a}{c} = \frac{bc + a}{c}, \quad b - \frac{a - x}{c} = \frac{bc - a + x}{c}$$

To find a fraction equivalent to a given mixed number, multiply the entire part by the denominator of the fraction, add, the numerator if the sign of the fraction be plus, subtract it if the sign be minus, and write the result over the denominator.

How may an entire number be changed to a fraction having a given denominator?

ILLUS. 3. Change $\frac{a}{b}$, $\frac{c}{d}$, and $\frac{x}{ab}$ to equivalent fractions having a common denominator.

$$\frac{a \times ad}{b \times ad} = \frac{a^2d}{abd}$$

$$\frac{c \times ab}{d \times ab} = \frac{abc}{abd}$$

$$\frac{x \times d}{ab \times d} = \frac{xd}{abd}$$

To change fractions to equivalent fractions having a common denominator, multiply the terms of each fraction by such a number as will make its denominator equal to the L.C.M. of the given denominators.

Exercise 43.

Change to equivalent entire or mixed numbers:

1. $\dfrac{bx - cx + m}{x}$

2. $\dfrac{mn + an + x}{n}$

3. $\dfrac{x^2 + y^2 + 3}{x - y}$

4. $\dfrac{a^3 + b^3 + 3}{x - y}$

5. $\dfrac{6a^3b^2c - 9a^2b^2 + 3c}{3a^2b}$

6. $\dfrac{6x^3y^2 + 10x^2y^2z - 2m}{2xy^2}$

7. $\dfrac{x^3 + 2x^2 - 2x + 1}{x^2 - x - 1}$

8. $\dfrac{2a^3 + a^2 - 2a + 1}{a^2 + a - 2}$

9. $\dfrac{x^3 + y^3}{x - y}$

10. $\dfrac{a^3 - b^3}{a + b}$

11. $\dfrac{8a^3}{2a-1}$

12. $\dfrac{27x^3}{3x+1}$

13. $\dfrac{3x^3+8x^2+2}{x^2+2x-1}$

14. $\dfrac{2a^3+3a^2+10a-4}{a^2+3a+2}$

15. $\dfrac{2a^4+6a^3-6a+2}{a^2+a-1}$

16. $\dfrac{3x^4-5x^3+x-1}{x^2-x-1}$

Change to equivalent fractions:

17. $x+y-\dfrac{xy}{x-y}$

18. $a-b-\dfrac{2ab}{a+b}$

19. $-c+d+\dfrac{c^3+d^3}{c^2+cd+d^2}$

20. $\dfrac{x^2y+xy^2}{x-y}+x^2-y^2$

21. $\dfrac{x+2}{3x-1}-x-2$

22. $2a-1-\dfrac{a-2}{a+3}$

23. $a^2-3a+2-\dfrac{a+3}{2a^2-1}$

24. $2x^2+x-3-\dfrac{x-2}{3x^2+1}$

25. $\dfrac{3x+2}{x^2+x+2}-1.$

26. $1-\dfrac{2a^2+3}{a^2-2a+3}.$

27. $\dfrac{a^2}{a^2-a+3}-a^2-a-1.$

28. $\dfrac{x^4}{x^2+x-1}-x^2+x-1.$

Change to equivalent fractions having a common denominator:

29. $\dfrac{a^2}{2}, \dfrac{xy}{3}, \dfrac{5ab^2}{4}.$

30. $\dfrac{x^3}{3}, \dfrac{am}{2}, \dfrac{3x^2y}{5}.$

31. $\dfrac{7x^2}{3y}, \dfrac{5xy}{2a}, \dfrac{x^3}{ay}.$

32. $\dfrac{2a^2}{7m}, \dfrac{5ab}{3n}, \dfrac{b^4}{mn}.$

33. $\dfrac{5}{y+x}, \dfrac{3x}{x-y}, \dfrac{2ab}{x^2-y^2}.$

34. $\dfrac{2}{3+a}, \dfrac{5a}{a-3}, \dfrac{2ax}{a^2-9}.$

35. $\dfrac{b^2}{a^2-ab}, \dfrac{a^2b}{a^2-b^2}.$

36. $\dfrac{m^3}{nm+n^2}, \dfrac{m^2n}{m^2-n^2}.$

37. $\dfrac{2}{x^4-y^4}, \dfrac{3}{x^2+xy-2y^2}.$

38. $\dfrac{5}{a^8-b^8}, \dfrac{2}{a^4-4a^2b^2+3b^4}.$

39. $\dfrac{a-1}{a^2-2a-15}, \dfrac{a+2}{a^2+a-6}, \dfrac{a+3}{a^2-7a+10}.$

40. $\dfrac{x+1}{x^2-x-6}, \dfrac{x-2}{x^2+6x+8}, \dfrac{x+2}{x^2+x-12}.$

41. $\dfrac{x^2+3x+2}{x^2-x-6}, \dfrac{x^2-x}{x^2+5x+4}, \dfrac{x^2-6x+9}{x^2+x-12}.$

42. If x quarts of milk cost m cents, what will one pint cost?

43. Express four consecutive numbers of which a is the largest.

44. What is the next even number above $2m$?

45. What is the next odd number below $4a+1$?

OPERATIONS UPON FRACTIONS.

ADDITION AND SUBTRACTION.

35. ILLUS. 1. Find the sum of $\frac{6a^2}{9x^2}$, $\frac{2a^2-a}{9x^2}$, and $-\frac{3a^2+1}{9x^2}$.

$$\frac{6a^2}{9x^2}+\frac{2a^2-a}{9x^2}+\left(-\frac{3a^2+1}{9x^2}\right)=\frac{6a^2+2a^2-a-3a^2-1}{9x^2}$$
$$=\frac{5a^2-a-1}{9x^2}$$

ILLUS. 2. Find the sum of $\frac{x}{xy-y^2}$, $\frac{1}{x-y}$, and $-\frac{1}{y}$.

$$\frac{x}{xy-y^2}+\frac{1}{x-y}+(-\frac{1}{y})=\frac{x}{y(x-y)}+\frac{y}{y(x-y)}-\frac{x-y}{y(x-y)}$$
$$=\frac{2y}{y(x-y)}=\frac{2}{x-y}$$

To add fractions, find equivalent fractions having a common denominator, add their numerators, write the sum over the common denominator, and reduce to lowest terms.

ILLUS. 3. Subtract $\frac{a-4b}{a-2b}$ from $\frac{a-2b}{a}$.

$$\frac{a-2b}{a}-\frac{a-4b}{a-2b}=\frac{a^2-4ab+4b^2}{a(a-2b)}-\frac{a^2-4ab}{a(a-2b)}=\frac{4b^2}{a(a-2b)}$$

Make a statement of the method of subtracting one fraction from another.

Exercise 44.

Find the value of:

1. $\frac{2a}{3}+\frac{a}{4}-\frac{5a}{6}$.
2. $\frac{2x}{5}+\frac{1}{3}x-\frac{2x}{3}$.
3. $\frac{2x}{3}-\frac{3x}{4}-\frac{4x}{5}$.
4. $\frac{4a}{b}+\frac{3x}{2m}$.
5. $\frac{2x}{3}-x+\frac{3x}{5}$.
6. $\frac{m^2}{n^2}-2+\frac{n^2}{m^2}$.

7. $\dfrac{x}{mn} - \dfrac{x+mn}{3n} + 2m.$

8. $\dfrac{2b+x}{3x} + \dfrac{5b-4x}{9x}.$

9. $\dfrac{3m-a}{am} + \dfrac{b-2m}{bm} - \dfrac{3b-2a}{ab}.$

10. $\dfrac{2a^2}{a^2-b^2} - \dfrac{2a}{a+b}.$

11. $\dfrac{2a-3b}{a-2b} - \dfrac{2a-b}{a-b}.$

12. $\dfrac{x+4}{x+5} - \dfrac{x+2}{x+3}.$

13. $\dfrac{x-4y}{x-2y} - \dfrac{x^2-4y^2}{x^2+2xy}.$

14. $\dfrac{x-7}{x+2} + \dfrac{x+4}{x-3}.$

15. $\dfrac{(x+2a)^2}{x^3-8a^3} - \dfrac{1}{x-2a}.$

16. $\dfrac{x^6+x^3y^3+y^6}{x^3+y^3} + \dfrac{x^6-x^3y^3+y^6}{x^3-y^3}.$

17. $\dfrac{m-3}{m+2} - \dfrac{m-2}{m+3} + \dfrac{1}{m-1}$

18. $\dfrac{2(4a+b)}{15a^2-15b^2} - \dfrac{1}{5(a+b)} - \dfrac{1}{3a-3b}$

19. $\dfrac{3x^3-3x^2+x-1}{3x^3-3x^2-x+1} - \dfrac{3x^3+3x^2-x-1}{3x^3+3x^2+x+1}$

20. $\dfrac{1}{a^2-7a+12} - \dfrac{1}{a^2-5a+6}$

21. $\dfrac{a-1}{a-2} + \dfrac{5-2a}{a^2-5a+6} + \dfrac{a-2}{a-3}$

22. $\dfrac{1}{a^2+3a+2} + \dfrac{2a}{a^2+4a+3} + \dfrac{1}{a^2+5a+6}$

23. $\dfrac{x+2}{x-5} + \dfrac{x-3}{x+4} - \dfrac{2x^2-3x-2}{x^2-x-20}$

24. $\dfrac{m-n}{mn} + \dfrac{p-m}{mp} + \dfrac{n-p}{np}$

25. $\dfrac{a+b}{ab}-\dfrac{a-c}{ac}-\dfrac{c-b}{bc}$

26. $\dfrac{x^2-yz}{(x+y)(x+z)}+\dfrac{x^2-xz}{(y+z)(y+x)}+\dfrac{z^2}{(z+x)(z+y)}$

27. $\dfrac{m^2-bx}{(m+b)(m+x)}-\dfrac{mx-b^2}{(b+x)(b+m)}-\dfrac{mb-x^2}{(x+m)(x+b)}$

28. x is how many times y?

29. If a is $\frac{2}{5}$ of a number, what is $\frac{1}{5}$ of the number?

30. If x is $\frac{3}{7}$ of a number, what is the number?

31. Seven years ago A was four times as old as B. If B is x years old, what is A's present age?

36. What is the effect of multiplying a number twice by -1? How many signs to a fraction?

Note carefully in the following illustrations the variety of changes that may be made in the signs without changing the value of the fraction:

ILLUS. 1.

$$\frac{a}{b}=\frac{-a}{-b}=-\frac{-a}{b}=-\frac{a}{-b}.$$

In case the terms of the fraction are polynomials, notice that the change in sign affects every term of the numerator or denominator.

ILLUS. 2.

$$\frac{a-b}{x-y}=\frac{b-a}{y-x}=-\frac{b-a}{x-y}=-\frac{a-b}{y-x}.$$

ILLUS. 3.

$$\frac{a-b+c}{x+y+z}=\frac{b-c-a}{-x-y-z}=-\frac{b-c-a}{x+y+z}=-\frac{a-b+c}{-x-y-z}$$

When the denominator of the fraction is expressed in its factors, the variety of changes is increased.

ILLUS. 4.

$$\begin{aligned}\frac{a}{(x-y)(m-n)}&=\frac{a}{(y-x)(n-m)}=\frac{-a}{(y-x)(m-n)}\\&=\frac{-a}{(x-y)(n-m)}=\frac{-a}{(x-y)(m-n)}\\&=\frac{a}{(y-x)(m-n)}=\frac{a}{(y-x)(n-m)}\end{aligned}$$

ILLUS. 5.

$$\frac{a-b}{(x-y)(c-d)} = \frac{b-a}{(y-x)(c-d)} = \frac{a-b}{(y-x)(d-c)}$$
$$= -\frac{a-b}{(y-x)(c-d)} = \text{etc.}$$

What is the effect on the value of a fraction of changing the signs of two factors of either denominator or numerator? Why? If the signs of only one factor of the denominator are changed, what must be done to keep the value of the fraction the same?

Write three equivalent fractions for each of the following by means of a change in the signs:

1. $\frac{xy}{mn}$

2. $\frac{3ab}{2x^3}$

3. $\frac{x+y}{a-b}$

4. $\frac{1-x}{3c-a^2}$

5. $\frac{x-y-x}{c+d-a}$

6. $\frac{3a-x+y^2}{m^2+2c^2d-z}$

Write six equivalent fractions for each of the following:

7. $\frac{x}{(a-b)(m-n)}$

8. $\frac{3a^2bc}{(2x-y)(a-z)}$

9. $\frac{a-m}{(c-d)(x-y)}$

10. $\frac{2c+d}{(a-b+c)(x-z)}$

Write as many equivalent fractions as possible for each of the following:

11. $\frac{c}{(a-b)(x-y)(m-n)}$

12. $\frac{a}{(c-d)(m-x)(y-b)}$

13. $\dfrac{a^2x}{(2m-n)(c-x)(d-y^2)}$

14. $\dfrac{(x-y)(2a-b)}{(m-x)(a-c)(d-y)}$

ILLUS. 1. Find the value of $\frac{1}{x+1} - \frac{1}{1-x} - \frac{x}{x^2-1}$.

$$\begin{aligned}\frac{1}{x+1} - \frac{1}{1-x} - \frac{x}{x^2-1} &= \frac{1}{x+1} + \frac{1}{x-1} - \frac{x}{x^2-1}\\ &= \frac{x-1}{x^2-1} + \frac{x+1}{x^2-1} - \frac{x}{x^2-1}\\ &= \frac{x}{x^2-1}\end{aligned}$$

ILLUS. 2. Find the value of $\frac{1}{(a-b)(b-c)} + \frac{1}{(b-a)(a-c)} + \frac{1}{(c-a)(c-b)}$.

$$\frac{1}{(a-b)(b-c)} + \frac{1}{(b-a)(a-c)} + \frac{1}{(c-a)(c-b)}$$

$$= \frac{1}{(a-b)(b-c)} - \frac{1}{(a-b)(a-c)} + \frac{1}{(a-c)(b-c)}$$

$$= \frac{a-c}{(a-b)(b-c)(a-c)} - \frac{b-c}{(a-b)(b-c)(a-c)} + \frac{a-b}{(a-b)(b-c)(a-c)}$$

$$= \frac{2a-2b}{(a-b)(b-c)(a-c)}$$

$$= \frac{2}{(b-c)(a-c)}$$

Exercise 45.

Find the value of:

1. $\dfrac{2x}{x^2-4} + \dfrac{1}{2-x} + \dfrac{1}{2+x}$.

2. $\dfrac{3a}{a^2-9} + \dfrac{1}{3-a} - \dfrac{1}{3+a}$.

3. $m^2 - \dfrac{am^2}{a-m} - \dfrac{am^2}{m+a} - \dfrac{2a^2m^2}{m^2-a^2}$.

4. $\dfrac{20a-4}{4a^2-1} + \dfrac{3}{1-2a} - \dfrac{6}{1-2a}$.

5. $\dfrac{1}{x-y} + \dfrac{3y^3}{y^3-x^3} - \dfrac{1}{3(1+a)}$.

6. $\dfrac{a+3}{6(a^2-1)} + \dfrac{1}{2(1-a)} + \dfrac{1}{3(1+a)}$.

7. $\dfrac{1}{5(3b-y^2)} - \dfrac{1}{2(3b+y^2)} - \dfrac{11b-7y^2}{10(y^4-9b^2)}$.

8. $\dfrac{3}{(1-x)(3-x)}+\dfrac{1}{(2-x)(x-3)}-\dfrac{1}{(x-1)(x-2)}$.

9. $\dfrac{a}{(a-b)(b-c)}+\dfrac{1}{c-a}-\dfrac{a-b}{(c-a)(c-b)}$.

10. $\dfrac{1}{(z-a)(z-y)}+\dfrac{1}{(a-z)(a-y)}+\dfrac{1}{(y-z)(y-a)}$.

11. $\dfrac{1}{(1-x)(1-y)}-\dfrac{x^2}{(x-1)(y-x)}-\dfrac{y^2}{(y-1)(x-y)}$.

12. $a-\dfrac{a^2}{a+1}-\dfrac{a}{1-a}$.

13. $1-a+a^2-a^3+\dfrac{a}{1+a}$.

14. $\dfrac{1}{x^2-7x+12}-\dfrac{2}{x^2-6x+8}+\dfrac{2}{x^2-5x+6}$.

15. What will a pounds of rice cost if b pounds costs 43 cents?

16. x is $\frac{4}{9}$ of what number?

17. m is $\frac{5}{x}$ of what number?

18. y is $\frac{a}{b}$ of what number?

MULTIPLICATION AND DIVISION.

37. ILLUS. $\dfrac{x^3}{y}\times c=\dfrac{x^3c}{y}$, $\dfrac{4x^y}{5a^2bc^3}\times ab=\dfrac{4x^2y}{5ac^3}$

A fraction is multiplied by multiplying the numerator or dividing the denominator.[5]

Exercise 46.

Multiply:

1. $\dfrac{a}{b^2}$ by x.

2. $\dfrac{3a^2bc}{7x^2y^3}$ by y^2.

3. $\dfrac{1}{2c^2d}$ by a^2d.

4. $\dfrac{4abc^2}{9x^2y}$ by $3xy$.

5. $\dfrac{3mn}{2x^2y^2}$ by $6x^2y$.

6. $\dfrac{x-y}{2mn}$ by $3x$.

7. $\dfrac{2a-b}{3x^2-xy}$ by x.

8. $\dfrac{x^2}{x^3-y^3}$ by $x-y$.

9. $\dfrac{3x+3y}{x-y}$ by x^2-y^2.

10. $\dfrac{a^2-4a-21}{a^2-3a-10}$ by $a-5$.

11. $x+y-\dfrac{4xy}{x+y}$ by $x+y$.

12. $a-b+\dfrac{4ab}{a-b}$ by $a-b$.

13. $\dfrac{1}{x-y+z}+\dfrac{2z}{(x-y)^2-z^2}$ by $x^2-xy-xz$.

14. $\dfrac{1}{a-b+c}-\dfrac{2b}{(a+c)^2-b^2}$ by $ac+bc+c^2$.

15. How many units of the value of $\frac{1}{5}$ are there in 2?

16. How many units of the value of $\frac{1}{x}$ are there in 5?

17. How many sixths are there in $4a$?

38. ILLUS. $\dfrac{xy^3}{2c}\div y^3=\dfrac{x}{3c},\dfrac{5abc}{3mn^2}$

A fraction is divided by dividing the numerator or multiplying the denominator.[6]

Exercise 47.

Divide:

1. $\dfrac{a^2x}{b}$ by ax.

---

[5]In arithmetic, which of these two methods did you find would apply to all examples? When either method may he applied to any given example, which is preferable, and why?

2. $\frac{3m^2n}{2xy}$ by $2x$.

3. $\frac{18cd^5}{5x}$ by $6cd^3$.

4. $\frac{6x^2y}{m}$ by $9mn$.

5. $\frac{a}{c+d}$ by $3x$.

6. $\frac{3x^3 - 3xy}{2m^2n}$ by $3x$.

7. $\frac{2ab - 2b^4}{5x^2yz}$ by $2ab$.

8. $\frac{5(a^2 - b^2)}{xy}$ by $a - b$.

9. $\frac{m + n}{2m^2 - 2mn}$ by $m^2 - n^2$.

10. $\frac{x^2 + 5x - 14}{x^2 - 7x + 12}$ by $x - 2$.

11. $ax + bx + a + b + \frac{a + b}{3x}$ by $a + b$.

12. Multiply $\frac{x^2 - 5x + 6}{x^2 + 3x - 4}$ by $x - 1$.

13. Divide $\frac{5bc^2}{6ax^3}$ by $10abc$.

14. Multiply $1 + \frac{3ac}{4x^2y}$ by $2ac$.

15. Divide $\frac{5x^2y - 5y^3}{2x^2z}$ by $4x + 4y$.

16. Divide $\frac{4x^2y}{3mn^2}$ by $6axy$.

17. A can do a piece of-work in $2\frac{1}{3}$ days, and B in $2\frac{1}{2}$ days. How much of the work can they both together do in one day?

18. If C can do a piece of work in m days, and D works half as fast as G, how much of the work can D do in one day?

[6]See previous foot-note.

39. ILLUS. 1. $\frac{x}{y} \times \frac{a}{4} = \frac{ax}{4y}$

ILLUS. 2. $\frac{7x^5y^4}{5a^3z^2} \times \frac{20a^2z^3}{42x^4y^3} = \frac{2xyz}{3a}$

ILLUS. 3. $\frac{ab - ax - 2b + 2x}{b^3 - x^3} \times \frac{b^2x + bx^2 + x^3}{a - 2}$

$$= \frac{(a-2)(b-x)x(b^2+bx+x^2)}{(b-x)(b^2+bx+x^2)(a-2)} = x$$

To multiply one fraction by another, multiply the numerators together for the numerator of the product and the denominators for its denominator, and reduce to lowest terms.

Exercise 48.

Simplify:

1. $\frac{7a^2b^2c}{18x^2y^2z} \times \frac{9xyz^2}{28abc^2}$

2. $\frac{9a^2b^2}{8nx^3y^2} \times \frac{5x^2y^2}{2am^2n} \times \frac{24m^2n^2x}{90ab^2}$

3. $\frac{x^2 - 16y^2}{xy - 4y^2} \times \frac{2y}{x + 4y}$

4. $\frac{3a - b}{2b} \times \frac{18ab + 6b^2}{9a^2 - b^2}$

5. $\frac{abd + cd^2}{a^2d - abc} \times \frac{acd - bc^2}{ab^2 + bcd}$

6. $\frac{2ax - 4y}{mn^2 + any} \times \frac{mny + ay^2}{a^2x - 2ay}$

7. $\frac{x^2 - x - 6}{x^2 + x - 2} \times \frac{x^2 + 3x - 4}{x^2 - 2x - 3}$

8. $\frac{a^2 + 2a - 3}{a^2 + a - 2} \times \frac{a^2 + 7a + 10}{a + 3}$

9. $\frac{x^4 - 64x}{3x^2 - 2x} \times \frac{9x^2 - 4}{x^2 - 4x}$

10. $\frac{m^2 - 25}{m^2 + 2m - 15} \times \frac{m^4 - 27m}{m^2 - 5m}$

11. $\frac{a^3 - a^2y + ay^2}{x - 3} \times \frac{ax + xy - 3a - 3y}{a^3 + y^3}$

12. $\dfrac{x^3+x^2-x-1}{x^2+6x+9} \times \dfrac{x^2+2x-3}{2x^3+4x^2+2x}$

13. $\dfrac{a^3-a^2-a+1}{a^2+4a+4} \times \dfrac{a^2+3a+2}{3a^3-6a^2+3a}$

14. $(m+\dfrac{mn}{m-n})(n-\dfrac{mn}{m+n})$

15. A grocer purchased y pounds of tea for \$25. Another grocer purchased 4 pounds less for the same money. What was the price per pound which each paid?

16. What is $\frac{a}{3}$ of $\frac{2}{c}$?

17. Two numbers differ by 28, and one is eight-ninths of the other. What are the numbers?

40. ILLUS. $\dfrac{b}{c} \div \dfrac{x}{y} = \dfrac{b}{c} \times \dfrac{y}{x} = \dfrac{by}{cx}$

To divide one fraction by another, invert the divisor and proceed as in multiplication.

Exercise 49.

Simplify:

1. $\dfrac{18a^6b^2c}{35x^3y^3z} \div \dfrac{3a^4b}{5x^2yz}$.

2. $\dfrac{7axy^2}{8m^2n} \div \dfrac{2xz^3}{3ab^2m}$.

3. $\dfrac{4x^2y^3z^4}{3a^2b^3c^4} \div \dfrac{3x^4y^3z^2}{4a^4b^3c^2}$.

4. $\dfrac{2am^3n^2}{3x^3yz^2} \div \dfrac{3a^3mn^2}{2x^3yz^2}$.

5. $\dfrac{x^2-7x+10}{x^2} \div \dfrac{x^2-4}{x^2+5x}$.

6. $\dfrac{x-6}{x-3} \div \dfrac{x^2-3x}{x^2-5x}$.

7. $\dfrac{x-2}{x-7} \div \dfrac{x^2-9x+20}{x^2-10x+21} \div \dfrac{x^2-4x+3}{x^2-5x+4}$.

8. $\dfrac{a^2-7a}{a-8} \div \dfrac{a^2+10a+24}{a^2-14a+48} \div \dfrac{a^2-7a+6}{a^2+3a-4}$.

9. $\frac{a+b}{(a-b)^2} div \frac{a^2+b^2}{a^2-b^2} \times \frac{a^4-b^4}{(a+b)^3}$.

10. $\frac{x^2-y^2}{x^2+y^2} \times \frac{x^4-y^4}{(x-y)^3} \div \frac{(x+y)^2}{x-y}$.

11. $\frac{a^2-2a-8}{a^2+2a-15} \div \frac{a^2+5a+6}{a^2-4a+3} \div \frac{a^2-5a+4}{a^2+8a+15}$.

12. $\frac{x^2-9x+20}{x^2-5x-14} \div \frac{x^2-7x+12}{x^2-x-42} \times \frac{x^2-x-6}{x^2+11x+30}$.

13. $\frac{a^2-a-2}{a^2+2a-8} \times \frac{a^2+5a}{ab+b} \div \frac{a^2-25}{a^2-a-20}$.

14. $\frac{m-2}{2m-14} \times \frac{m^2-5m-14}{2m^2+4m} \times \frac{4m^2}{m^2-4} \div \frac{2mn-14n}{m^2-5m-14}$.

15. $\left(\frac{a+1}{a-1}+1\right)\left(\frac{a-1}{a+1}+1\right) \div \left(\frac{a+1}{a-1}-1\right)\left(1-\frac{a-1}{a+1}\right)$.

16. $\left(1+\frac{x}{1-x}\right)\left(1-\frac{x}{1+x}\right) \div \left(1+\frac{1+x}{1-x}\right)\left(1-\frac{1-x}{1+x}\right)$.

17. How much times 7 is 21?

18. How much times $\frac{3}{14}$ is $\frac{6}{7}$?

19. How much times $\frac{c}{d}$ is $\frac{x}{4}$?

20. How much times $\frac{5bz}{7mx^3}$ is $\frac{3xy^2z}{4amn^2}$?

What may be done to a fraction without changing its value? How multiply a fraction? When is a fraction in its lowest terms? How reduce a fraction to lowest terms? How divide one fraction by another? How add fractions? How divide a fraction? What is the effect of increasing the denominator of a fraction? What is the effect of dividing the numerator of a fraction? What is the effect of subtracting from the denominator of a fraction? How multiply two or more fractions together? What is the effect of adding to the numerator of a fraction? What is the effect of multiplying a fraction by its denominator? What changes in the signs of a fraction can be made without changing the value of the fraction? How change an entire number to a fraction with a given denominator?

INVOLUTION, EVOLUTION, AND FACTORING.

41. ILLUS. 1. $\left(\frac{a}{b}\right)^2 = \frac{a}{b} \times \frac{a}{b} = \frac{a^2}{b^2}$.

What is the square of $\frac{3x}{2y}$? What is the cube of $\frac{x}{y}$? of $\frac{2a^2b}{xy}$? What is the square root of $\frac{64x^2}{9y^4}$? What is the cube root of $\frac{8a^3x^6}{27b^9y^3}$? How find any power of a fraction? How find any root of a fraction?

ILLUS. 2. $\left(\frac{m}{n}+\frac{1}{x}\right)\left(\frac{m}{n}-\frac{1}{x}\right)=\frac{m^2}{n^2}-\frac{1}{x^2}$.

ILLUS. 3. $\left(\frac{x}{y}-3\right)\left(\frac{x}{y}-6\right)=\frac{x^2}{y^2}-\frac{9x}{y}+18$.

ILLUS. 4. Factor $\frac{b^4}{a^4}-\frac{y^4}{x^4}$.

$$\frac{b^4}{a^4}-\frac{y^4}{x^4}=\left(\frac{b^2}{a^2}+\frac{y^2}{x^2}\right)\left(\frac{b}{a}+\frac{y}{x}\right)\left(\frac{b}{a}-\frac{y}{x}\right).$$

ILLUS. 5. Factor $x^4+x^3+\frac{1}{4}$.

$$x^4+x^2+\frac{1}{4}=\left(x^2+\frac{1}{2}\right)^2.$$

Exercise 50.

Find by inspection the values of each of the following:

1. $\left(\frac{2x^2}{ab^3}\right)^2$.

2. $\left(\frac{a^2b^3}{4y}\right)^3$.

3. $\left(-\frac{2xy}{3a^2m^3}\right)^5$).

4. $\left(\frac{x(a-b)}{3a^2b}\right)^4$.

5. $\left(-\frac{5x^2y(a+b^2)^2}{2ab^3(x^2-y)^3}\right)^3$.

6. $\left(-\frac{3am^4(2a+3b)^3}{4x^2y^2(m-n)^2}\right)^3$.

7. $\left(-\frac{3a^5xy^2z^3}{2bc^4d^4}\right)^4$.

8. $\left(-\frac{4x^7y^2z^3}{3ab^6d^3}\right)^4$.

9. $\sqrt[3]{\frac{8a^3b^6}{27m^6n^9}}$.

10. $\sqrt{\dfrac{36m^2n^8}{121a^4b^6}}$.

11. $\sqrt[4]{\dfrac{256x^4y^8}{81a^4b^{12}}}$.

12. $\sqrt[5]{-\dfrac{32x^5y^10}{243m^10n^15}}$.

13. $\sqrt[3]{-\dfrac{27x^6(a-b)^9}{64a^6b^{12}}}$.

14. $\sqrt{\dfrac{4x^2+12xy+9y^2}{16x^4y^8}}$.

15. $\sqrt{\dfrac{8x^2(x+y)^5}{50y^4(x+y)}}$.

16. $\sqrt[3]{-\dfrac{81a^3(a-b)^7}{24b^9(a-b)}}$.

17. $\left(\dfrac{x}{y}+\dfrac{a}{b}\right)\left(\dfrac{x}{y}-\dfrac{a}{b}\right)$.

18. $\left(\frac{a}{b}-\frac{c}{d}\right)\left(\frac{a}{b}+\frac{c}{d}\right)$.

19. $3ab\left(\dfrac{2x}{ab}+\dfrac{x^2}{2mn}-\dfrac{ax}{3mb}\right)$.

20. $\dfrac{x^2}{yz}\left(\dfrac{2x}{3}-\dfrac{3y^2z}{2x}+\dfrac{x^2y}{m^2z}\right)$.

21. $\left(\dfrac{a^4}{b^4}+\dfrac{c^4}{d^4}\right)\left(\dfrac{a^2}{b^2}+\dfrac{c^2}{d^2}\right)\left(\frac{a}{b}+\frac{c}{d}\right)\left(\frac{a}{b}-\frac{c}{d}\right)$.

22. $\left(\dfrac{x^2}{16}+\dfrac{9y^2}{25m^1}\right)\left(\dfrac{x}{4}+\dfrac{3y}{5m}\right)\left(\dfrac{x}{4}-\dfrac{3y}{5m}\right)$.

23. $\left(\dfrac{x}{y}+1\right)\left(\dfrac{x^2}{y^2}-\dfrac{x}{y}+1\right)$.

24. $\left(\frac{a}{b}-1\right)\left(\dfrac{a^2}{b^2}+\dfrac{a}{b}+1\right)$.

25. $\left(\dfrac{x}{y}-\dfrac{3a^2}{2b}\right)$.

26. $\left(\frac{2y}{c^2} + \frac{9}{2d}\right)^2.$

27. $\left(\frac{a}{b} + 2\right)\left(\frac{a}{b} - 5\right).$

28. $\left(\frac{x}{y} - \frac{a}{b}\right)^3.$

Factor:

29. $\frac{x^4}{a^2} - \frac{b^2}{y^4}$

30. $\frac{a^2}{b^4} - \frac{x^8}{y^2}$

31. $\frac{a^4}{m^4} - \frac{b^4}{x^4}$

32. $\frac{8a^3}{y^3} + \frac{b^3}{c^3}$

33. $\frac{x^3}{27a^3} - \frac{y^3}{c^3}$

34. $\frac{81a^4}{b^4} - \frac{x^4y^4}{625z^4}$

35. $\frac{m^2}{y^2} + \frac{2m}{y} - 15$

36. $\frac{x^2}{a^2} - \frac{2x}{a} - 8$

37. $\frac{y^2}{4} + 2 + \frac{4}{y^2}$

38. $\frac{x^2}{a^2} + \frac{a^2}{x^2} - 2$

39. A dog can take 2 leaps of a feet each in a second. How many feet can he go in 9 seconds?

40. How many weeks would it take to build a stone wall if $\frac{1}{a}$ of it can be built in one day?

COMPLEX FRACTIONS.

42 ILLUS. $\dfrac{a+\frac{b}{c}}{d}$, $\dfrac{a}{d-\frac{x}{y}}$, $\dfrac{a+\frac{b}{c}}{d-\frac{x}{y}}$, $\dfrac{\frac{a}{x}}{\frac{b}{c}}$

A **complex fraction** is one which has a fraction in one or both of its terms.

What is a simple fraction? What is the effect of multiplying a simple fraction by its denominator or by any multiple of its denominator? By what must the numerator of the complex fraction $\dfrac{a+\frac{ax}{b}}{\frac{c}{d}+\frac{x}{ab}}$ be multiplied to make the numerator an entire number? By what multiply the denominator to make it an entire number? If both numerator and denominator are multiplied, under what conditions will the value of the fraction remain the same?

ILLUS. 1. Simplify $\dfrac{a+\frac{ax}{b}}{\frac{c}{d}+\frac{x}{ab}}$.

$$\frac{a+\frac{ax}{b}\times abd}{\frac{c}{d}+\frac{x}{ab}\times abd}=\frac{a^2bd+a^2dx}{abc+dx}$$

ILLUS. 2. Simplify $\dfrac{\frac{1}{1-x}-\frac{1}{1+x}}{\frac{1}{1-x}+\frac{1}{1+x}}$.

$$\frac{\frac{1}{1-x}-\frac{1}{1+x}\times(1-x)(1+x)}{\frac{1}{1-x}+\frac{1}{1+x}\times(1-x)(1+x)}=\frac{1+x-1+x}{1+x+1-x}=\frac{2x}{2}=x$$

To simplify a complex fraction, multiply each term of the complex fraction by the L.C.M. of the denominators of the fractions in the terms, and reduce.

Exercise 51.

Simplify:

1. $\dfrac{1+\frac{a}{b}}{\frac{x}{b}-1}$.

2. $\dfrac{x+\frac{a}{y}}{m-\frac{b}{y}}$.

3. $\dfrac{x}{a+\frac{b}{c}}$.

4. $\dfrac{x-\frac{1}{x^2}}{1-\frac{1}{x}}$.

5. $\dfrac{\frac{a}{b}-\frac{b}{a}}{a-b}$.

6. $\dfrac{1+m^3}{1+\frac{1}{m}}$.

7. $\dfrac{\frac{x}{y}-\frac{z}{x}}{\frac{a}{y}-\frac{b}{x}}$.

8. $\dfrac{\frac{ab}{c}-3d}{3c-\frac{ab}{d}}$.

9. $\dfrac{1+\frac{1}{a-1}}{1-\frac{1}{a+1}}$.

10. $\frac{1+a+a^2}{1+\frac{1}{a}+\frac{1}{a^2}}$.

11. $\dfrac{x-3-\frac{2}{x-4}}{x-1+\frac{2}{x-4}}$.

12. $\dfrac{\frac{a}{a+b}+\frac{a}{a-b}}{\frac{2a}{a^2-b^2}}$.

13. $\dfrac{\frac{a+1}{a-1}+\frac{a-1}{a+1}}{\frac{a+1}{a-1}-\frac{a-1}{a+1}}$.

14. $\dfrac{\frac{a^3+b^3}{a^2-b^2}}{\frac{a^2-ab+b^2}{a-b}}$.

15. $1-\dfrac{1}{1+\frac{2}{a-2}}$.

16. $\dfrac{\frac{a+2b}{b}-\frac{a}{a+b}}{\frac{a+2b}{a+b}+\frac{a}{b}}$.

17. How many pounds of pepper can be bought for y dollars, if x pounds cost $2x$ dimes?

18. How many inches in y feet? How many yards?

19. A man bought x pounds of beef at x cents a pound, and handed the butcher a y-dollar bill. How many cents change should he receive?

20. x times I is how many times m?

Exercise 52. (Review.)

1. Divide $x^3-19x+6x^7+20+8x^2+16x^4-x^6-11x^5$ by $x^2+4-3x+2x^3$.

2. Find two numbers whose sum is 100 and whose difference is 10.

3. Find the G.C.F. of x^4-1, $x^5+x^4-x^3-x^2+x+1$, and x^2-x-2.

4. Factor $x^{10}-14x^5y+49y^2$, a^9-b^9, $3a^2-3a-216$.

5. Reduce $\dfrac{(2a+2b)(a^2-b^2)}{(a^2+2ab+b^2)(a-b)}$ to lowest terms.

6. Factor $\dfrac{16x^4}{a^4b^4} - \dfrac{c^4}{81y^4}$.

7. If x and y stand for the digits of a number of two places, what will represent the number?

8. Find the L.C.M. of a^2-5a+6, a^2-16, a^2-9, $a^2-7a+12$, and a^2-4.

9. If one picture costs a cents, how many can be bought for x dollars?

Simplify:

10. $\dfrac{x-3}{x-2} + \dfrac{2(1-x)}{x^2-6x+8} - \dfrac{x-1}{x-4}$.

11. $\dfrac{1}{(2-x)(3-x)} - \dfrac{2}{(x-1)(x-3)} + \dfrac{1}{(x-1)(x-2)}$.

12. $\dfrac{x^2+xy}{x-y} \times \dfrac{x^3-3x^2y+3xy^2-y^3}{x^2-y^2} \div \dfrac{2xy-2y^2}{3}$.

13. $\left(\dfrac{1}{m}+\dfrac{1}{n}\right)(a+b) - \left(\dfrac{a+b}{m}\right) - \left(\dfrac{a-b}{n}\right)$.

14. $\left(x - \dfrac{1}{1+\frac{2}{x-1}}\right) \div \dfrac{x+\frac{1}{x}}{\frac{1}{x}+1}$.

15. $\dfrac{\frac{a}{b}+\frac{b}{a}-1}{\frac{a^2}{b^2}+\frac{a}{b}+1} \times \dfrac{1+\frac{b}{a}}{a-b} \div \dfrac{1+\frac{b^3}{a^3}}{\frac{a^2}{b}-\frac{b^2}{a}}$.

16. Prove that $3(a+b)(a+c)(b+c) = (a+b+c)^3 - (a^3+b^3+c^3)$.

17. How many sevenths in $6xy$?

18. Divide $2x^5 - \dfrac{x^4}{12} + 2\dfrac{3}{4}x^3 - 2x^2 - x$ by $3x^2+x$.

EQUATIONS

43. ILLUS. 1. $27 + 10x = 13x + 23.$

ILLUS. 2. $\dfrac{a^2}{x} + \dfrac{b}{2} = \dfrac{4b^2}{x} + \dfrac{a}{4}.$

An **equation** is an expression of the equality of two numbers. The parts of the expression separated by the sign of equality are called the **members** of the equation.

The last letters of the alphabet are used to represent unknown numbers, and known numbers are represented by figures or by the first letters of the alphabet.

44. ILLUS. 1. $5x + 20 = 105.$

$5x = 85.$

ILLUS. 2. $3x - 18 = 42.$

$3x = 60.$

ILLUS. 3. $\frac{x}{12} = 2.$

$x = 24.$

ILLUS. 4. $7x = 49.$

$x = 7.$

Any changes may be made in an equation which do not destroy the equality of the members.

Name some of the ways in which such changes may be made.

45. ILLUS. 1. $x + b = a$. Subtracting b from each member, $x = a - b$.

ILLUS. 2. $x - b = c$. Adding b to each member, $x = c + b$.

In each of these illustrations b has been transposed (changed over) from the first to the second member, and in each case its sign has been changed. Hence,

Any term may be transposed from one member of an equation to the other provided its sign be changed.

46. ILLUS. $\dfrac{ab + x}{b^2} - \dfrac{b^2 - x}{a^2 b} = \dfrac{x - b}{a^2} - \dfrac{ab - x}{b^2}.$

Multiply both members by a^2b^2,

$$a^3b + a^2x - b^3 + bx = b^2x - b^3 - a^3b + a^2x.$$

To clear an equation of fractions, multiply each member of the equation by the L.C.M. of the denominators of the fractional terms.

47. ILLUS. 1. Solve

$$\begin{aligned} x+4+2(x-1) &= 3x+4-(5x-8) \\ x+5+2x-2 &= 3x+4-5x-8 \\ \text{Transposing, } x+2x-3x+5x &= 4+8-4+2 \\ 5x &= 10 \\ x &= 2 \end{aligned}$$

ILLUS. 2. Solve $\frac{5x+3}{8}-\frac{3-4x}{3}+\frac{x}{2}=\frac{31}{2}-\frac{9-5x}{6}$. Multiply by 24,

$$\begin{aligned} 3(5x+3)-8(3-4x)+12x &= 372-4(9-5x) \\ 15x+9-24+32x+12x &= 372-36+20x \\ \text{Transposing, } 15x+32x+12x-20x &= 372-36-9+24 \\ 39x &= 351 \\ x &= 9 \end{aligned}$$

To solve an equation, clear of fractions if necessary, transpose the terms containing the unknown number to one member and the known terms to the other, unite the terms, and divide both members by the coefficient of the unknown number.

Exercise 53.

Solve:

1. $22-6x=34-12x$.
2. $5x-4=10x+11$.
3. $23-8x=80-11x$.
4. $5x-21=7x+5$.
5. $18x-43=17-6x$.
6. $18-8x=12x-87$.
7. $9x-(2x-5)=4x+(13+x)$.
8. $15x-2(5x-4)-39=0$.
9. $12x-18x+17=8x+3$.
10. $21x-57=6x-14x+30$.
11. $5x-27-11x+16=98-40x-41$.

12. $14(x-2)+3(x+1)=2(x-5)$.

13. $6(23-x)-3x=3(4x-27)$.

14. $3(x-1)-2(x-3)+(x-2)-5=0$.

15. $(x+5)(x-3)=(x+2)(x-5)$.

16. $(x+4)(x+7)=(x+2)(x+11)$.

17. $(x-1)(x+4)(x-2)=x(x-2)(x+2)$.

18. $(x-5)(x+3)-(x-7)(x-2)-2(x-1)=-12$.

19. $(x+2)^2-(x-1)^2=5(2x+3)$.

20. $(2x+3)(x+3)-14=(2x+1)(x+1)$.

21. $(x+1)^2+(x-5)^2=2(x+5)^2$.

22. $7x-15+4x-6=4x-9-9x$.

23. Divide the number 105 into three parts, such that the second shall be 5 more than the first, and the third three times the second.

24. A man had a certain amount of money; he earned four times as much the next week, and found \$30. If he then had seven times as much as at first, how much had he at first?

25. How many fourths are there in $7x$?

26. How long will it take a man to build x yards of wall if he builds z feet a day?

27. $6x-\dfrac{x+4}{3}=\dfrac{x}{3}+28$.

28. $\dfrac{2x-1}{5}-\dfrac{x+12}{3}-4\dfrac{4}{5}=\dfrac{2x}{3}$.

29. $x-\dfrac{x}{4}+25=\dfrac{x}{3}+\dfrac{x}{2}+21$.

30. $\dfrac{x-3}{3}+\dfrac{5}{21}=-\dfrac{x-8}{7}$.

31. $\dfrac{8-5x}{12}+\dfrac{5x-6}{4}-\dfrac{7x+5}{6}=0$.

32. $\dfrac{3+5x}{4}+\dfrac{x+2}{2}=1\dfrac{5}{9}$.

33. $\dfrac{2x-1}{3}-\dfrac{13}{42}=\dfrac{5x-4}{6}$.

34. $\dfrac{1-11x}{7}-\dfrac{7x}{13}=\dfrac{2}{13}-\dfrac{8x-15}{3}$.

35. $\dfrac{2}{x}-\dfrac{3}{2x}=\dfrac{7}{24}-\dfrac{2}{3x}$.

36. $\dfrac{1}{4}+\dfrac{1}{3x}=\dfrac{11}{36}+\dfrac{1}{6x}$.

37. $\dfrac{3}{4x}-\dfrac{2}{x}+\dfrac{x-2}{2x}+7\dfrac{5}{12}=5+\dfrac{4}{6x}$.

38. $\dfrac{2x+3}{5x}-\dfrac{3}{x}+4=\dfrac{1}{2x}+\dfrac{3}{4x}+2\dfrac{23}{40}$.

39. $\dfrac{x+9}{11}-\dfrac{2-x}{5}=\dfrac{x+5}{7}$.

40. $\dfrac{x+4}{5}-\dfrac{4-x}{7}=\dfrac{x+1}{3}$.

41. $\dfrac{2}{5}(x-6)-\dfrac{3}{16}(x-1)=\dfrac{5}{12}(4-x)-\dfrac{5}{48}$.

42. $\dfrac{4+x}{4}-\dfrac{1-x}{7}-\dfrac{1}{5}(8-x)=\dfrac{x-23}{5}+7$.

43. How long will it take a man to walk x miles if he walks 15 miles in b hours?

44. What is the interest on m dollars for one year at 5 per cent?

45. What are the two numbers whose sum is 57, and whose difference is 25?

46. What is the interest on b dollars for y years at 4 per cent?

47. $(c+a)x+(c-b)x=c^2$.

48. $(a-b)x+(a+b)x=a$.

49. $2x+a(x-2)=a+6$.

50. $b(2x-a)-a^2=2x(a+b)-3ab$.

51. $a^2+c^2=\dfrac{cx}{a}+\dfrac{ax}{c}$.

52. $b^4-x^2+2bx=(b^2+x)(b^2-x)$.

53. $x^2+4a^2+a^4=\left(x+a^2\right)^2$.

54. $b^2(x-b)+a^2(x-a)=abx$.

55. $\dfrac{2x+5}{5x+3}=\dfrac{2x-4}{5x-6}$.

56. $\dfrac{6x+5}{2x-3}=\dfrac{3x-4}{x+1}$.

57. $\dfrac{2+9x}{3(6x+7)} = \dfrac{2x+9}{35+4x}$.

58. $\dfrac{3}{2-5x} - \dfrac{4}{1-3x} = 0$.

59. $\dfrac{2(3x+4)}{1+2x} - 1 = \dfrac{2(19+x)}{x+12}$.

60. $1 - \dfrac{x}{x+2} = \dfrac{4}{x+6}$.

61. $\dfrac{x^2}{1-x^2} + \dfrac{x+1}{x-1} = \dfrac{3}{x+1}$.

62. $\dfrac{2+3x}{1-x} + 5 = \dfrac{2x-4}{x+2}$.

63. $\dfrac{5}{6+2x} + \dfrac{2}{x+1} = \dfrac{2\frac{1}{2}}{2+2x} + \dfrac{4}{3+x}$.

64. $\dfrac{2(1-2x)}{1-3x} + \dfrac{1}{6} = \dfrac{1-3x}{1-2x}$.

65. $\dfrac{x-8}{x-6} - \dfrac{x}{x-2} = \dfrac{x-9}{x-7} - \dfrac{x+1}{x-1}$.

66. $\dfrac{x+5}{x+8} - \dfrac{x+6}{x+9} = \dfrac{x+2}{x+5} - \dfrac{x+3}{x+6}$.

67. Find three consecutive numbers whose sum is 81.

68. A's age is double B's, B's is three times C's, and C is y years old. What is A's age?

69. How many men will be required to do in a hours what x men do in 6 hours?

70. Find the sum of three consecutive odd numbers of which the middle one is $4x+1$.

Exercise 54

.

1. In a school of 836 pupils there is one boy to every three girls. How many are there of each?

2. Divide 253 into three parts, so that the first part shall be four times the second, and the second twice the third.

3. The sum of the ages of two brothers is 44 years, and one of them is 12 years older than the other. Find their ages.

4. Find two numbers whose sum is 158, and whose difference is 86.

5. Henry and Susan picked 16 quarts of berries. Henry picked 4 quarts less than three times as many as Susan. How many quarts did each pick?

6. Divide 127 into three parts, such that the second shall be 5 more than the first, and the third four times the second.

7. Twice a certain number added to four times the double of that number is 90. What is the number?

8. I bought some five-cent stamps, and twice as many two-cent stamps, paying for the whole 81 cents. How many stamps of each kind did I buy?

9. Three barns contain 58 tons of hay. In the first barn there are 3 tons more than in the second, and 7 less than in the third. How many tons in each barn?

10. If I add 18 to a certain number, five times this second number will equal eleven times the original number. What is the original number?

11. In a mixture of 48 pounds of coffee there is one-third as much Mocha as Java. How much is there of each?

12. The half and fifth of a number are together equal to 56. What is the number?

13. What number increased by one-third and one-fourth of itself, and 7 more, equals 45?

14. What number is doubled by adding to it three-eighths of itself, one-third of itself, and 14?

15. A grocer sold 27 pounds of sugar, tea, and meal. Of meal he sold 3 pounds more than of tea, and of sugar 6 pounds more than of meal. How many pounds of each did he sell?

16. A son is two-sevenths as old as his father. If the sum of their ages is 45 years, how old is each?

17. Two men invest $2990 in business, one putting in four-ninths as much as the other. How much does each invest?

18. In an election 47,519 votes were cast for three candidates. One candidate received 2061 votes less, and the other 1546 votes less, than the winning candidate. How many votes did each receive?

19. John had twice as many stamps as Ralph, but after he had bought 65, and Ralph had lost 16, they found that they had together 688. How many had each at first?

20. Find three consecutive numbers whose sum is 192.

21. If 17 be added to the sum of two numbers whose difference is 12, the result will be 61. What are the numbers?

22. Divide 120 into two parts such that five times one part may be equal to three times the other.

23. Mr. Johnson is twice as old as his son; 12 years ago he was three times as old. What is the age of each?

24. Henry is six times as old as his sister, but in 3 years from now he will be only three times as old. How old is each?

25. Samuel is 16 years older than James; 4 years ago he was three times as old. How old is each?

26. Martha is 5 years old and her father is 30. In how many years will her father be twice as old as Martha?

27. George is three times as old as Amelia; in 6 years his age will be twice hers. What is the age of each?

28. Esther is three-fourths as old as Edward; 20 years ago she was half as old. What is the age of each?

29. Mary is 4 years old and Flora is 9. In how many will Mary be two-thirds as old as Flora?

30. Harry is 9 years older than his little brother; in 6 years he will be twice as old. How old is each?

31. Divide $2x^4 + 27xy^3 - 81y^4$ by $x + 3y$.

32. Prove $\left(a^2 + ab + b^2\right)^2 - \left(a^2 - ab + b^2\right)^2 = 4ab(a^2 + b^2)$.

33. Find the value of $\dfrac{x-y}{y} + \dfrac{2x}{x-y} - \dfrac{x^3 + x^2y}{x^2y - y^3}$.

34. Solve $\dfrac{5x-7}{2} - 3x = \dfrac{2x+7}{3} - 14$.

35. Mr. Ames has \$132, and Mr. Jones \$43. How much must Mr. A. give to Mr. J. so that Mr. J. may have three-fourths as much as Mr. A.?

36. A has \$101, and B has \$35; each loses a certain sum, and then A has four times as much as B. What was the sum lost by each?

37. A certain sum of money was divided among A, B, and C; A and B received \$75, A and C \$108, and B and C \$89. How much did each receive?

Suggestion. Let x equal what A received.

38. Mary and Jane have the same amount of money. If Mary should give Jane 40 cents, she would have one-third as much as Jane. What amount of money has each?

39. An ulster and a suit of clothes cost \$43; the ulster and a hat cost \$27; the suit of clothes and the hat cost \$34. How much did each cost?

40. John, Henry, and Arthur picked berries, and sold them; John and Henry received \$4.22, John and Arthur \$3.05, Henry and Arthur \$3.67. How much did each receive for his berries?

41. A can do a piece of work in 4 days, and B can do it in 6 days. In what time can they do it working together?

Suggestion. Let x equal the required time. Then find what part of the work each can do in one day.

42. Mr. Brown can build a stone wall in 10 days, and Mr. Mansfield in 12 days. How long would it take them to do it working together?

43. Mr. Richards and his son can hoe a field of corn in 9 hours, but it takes Mr. Richards alone 15 hours. How long would it take the son to hoe the field?

44. A can do a piece of work in 4 hours, B can do it in 6 hours, and C in 3 hours. How long would it take them working together?

45. A can mow a field in 6 hours, B in 8 hours, and with the help of C they can do it in 2 hours. How long would it take C working alone?

46. A tank can be emptied by two pipes in 5 hours and 7 hours respectively. In what time can it be emptied by the two pipes together?

47. A cistern can be filled by two pipes in 4 hours and 6 hours respectively, and can be emptied by a third in 15 hours. In what time could the cistern be filled if all three pipes were running?

48. A and B together can do a piece of work in 8 days, A and C together in 10 days, and A by himself in 12 days. In what time can B and C do it? In what time can A, B, and C together do it?

49. John and Henry can together paint a fence in 2 hours, John and Lewis together in 4 hours, and John by himself in 6 hours. In what time can the three together do the painting?

50. C can do a piece of work in a days, and D can do the same work in b days. In how many days can they do it working together?

51. James and Thomas can do a piece of work in d days and James alone can do it in c days. How long would it take Thomas alone?

52. Solve $\dfrac{3+x}{3-x} - \dfrac{1+x}{1-x} - \dfrac{2+x}{2-x} = 1.$

53. Find the value of $\dfrac{x^2}{(x-y)(x-z)} + \dfrac{y^2}{(y-x)(y-z)} + \dfrac{z^2}{(z-x)(z-y)}.$

54. Expand $(x^2-2)(x^2+2)(x^2+3)(x^2-3)$.

55. Factor $9a^2+12ab+4b^2$, $12+7x+x^2$, $ac-2bc-3ad+6bd$.

Illustrative Example. At what time between 1 o'clock and 2 o'clock are the hands of a clock (1) together? (2) at right angles? (3) opposite to each other?

How far does the hour hand move while the minute hand goes around the whole circle? How far while the minute hand goes half around? What part of the distance that the minute hand moves in a given time does the hour hand move in the same time?

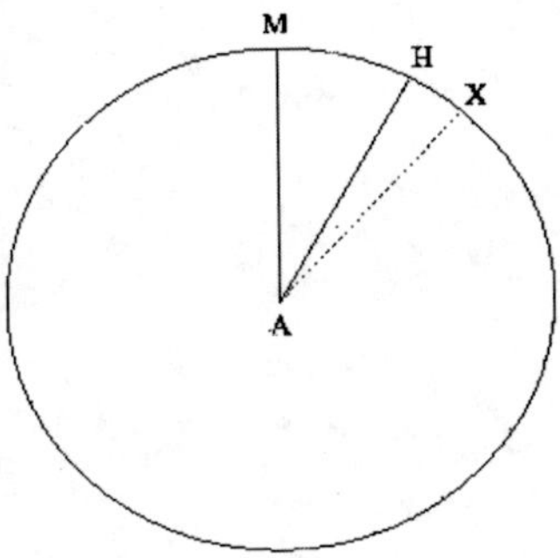

Figure 1:

(1) Let AM and AH in all the figures denote the positions of the minute and hour hands at 1 o'clock, and AX (Fig. 1) the position of both hands when together.

Let $\quad x =$ number of minute spaces in arc MX.

$$MX = MH + HX.$$

$$x = 5 + \tfrac{x}{12}. \text{ Solution gives } x = 5\tfrac{5}{11}.$$

Hence, the time is $5\frac{5}{11}$ minutes past 1 o'clock.

(2) Let AX and AB (Fig. 2) denote the positions of the minute and hour hands when at right angles.

Let $\quad x =$ number of minute spaces in arc MBX.

$$MBX = MH + HB + BX.$$

$$x = 5 + \tfrac{x}{12} + 15. \text{ Solution gives } x = 21\tfrac{9}{11}.$$

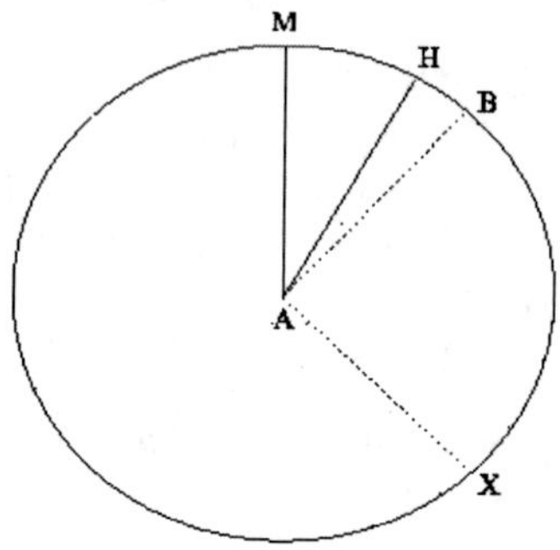

Figure 2:

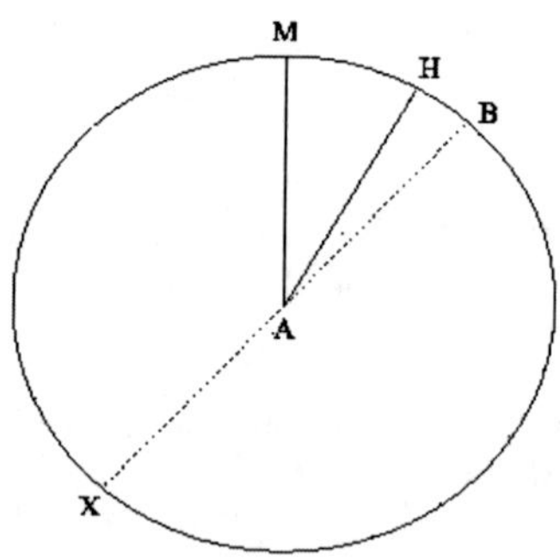

Figure 3:

Hence, the time is $21\frac{9}{11}$ minutes past 1 o'clock.

(3) Let AX and AB (Fig. 3) denote the positions of the minute and hour hands when opposite.

$$\begin{aligned} \text{Let} \qquad x &= \text{number of minute spaces in arc } MBX. \\ MBX &= MH + HB + BX. \\ x &= 5 + \tfrac{x}{12} + 30. \text{ Solution gives } x = 38\tfrac{2}{11}. \end{aligned}$$

Hence, the time is $38\frac{2}{11}$ minutes past 1 o'clock.

56. At what time are the hands of a clock together between 2 and 3? Between 5 and 6? Between 9 and 10?

57. At what time are the hands of a clock at right angles between 2 and 3? Between 4 and 5? Between 7 and 8?

58. At what time are the hands of a clock opposite each other between 3 and 4? Between 8 and 9? Between 12 and 1?

59. At what times between 4 and 5 o'clock are the hands of a watch ten minutes apart?

60. At what time between 8 and 9 o'clock are the hands of a watch 25 minutes apart?

61. At what time between 5 and 6 o'clock is the minute hand three minutes ahead of the hour hand?

62. It was between 12 and 1 o'clock; but a man, mistaking the hour hand for the minute hand, thought that it was 55 minutes later than it really was. What time was it?

63. At what time between 11 and 12 o'clock are the hands two minutes apart?

Illustrative Example. A courier who travels at the rate of 6 miles an hour is followed, 5 hours later, by another who travels at the rate of $8\frac{1}{2}$ miles an hour. In how many hours will the second overtake the first?

$$\begin{aligned} \text{Let} \qquad x &= \text{number of hours the second is traveling.} \\ x + 5 &= \text{number of hours the first is traveling.} \\ 8\tfrac{1}{2}x &= \text{distance the second travels.} \\ 6(x+5) &= \text{distance the first travels.} \\ 8\tfrac{1}{2}x &= 6(x+5). \text{ Solution gives } x = 12. \end{aligned}$$

He will overtake the first in 12 hours.

64. A messenger who travels at the rate of 10 miles an hour is followed, 4 hours later, by another who travels at the rate of 12 miles an hour. How long will it take the second to overtake the first?

65. A courier who travels at the rate of 19 miles in 4 hours is followed, 8 hours later, by another who travels at the rate of 19 miles in 3 hours. In what time will the second overtake the first? How far will the first have gone before he is overtaken?

66. A train going at the rate of 20 miles an hour is followed, on a parallel track, 4 hours later, by an express train. The express overtakes the first train in $5\frac{1}{3}$ hours. What is the rate of the express train?

67. A messenger started for Washington at the rate of $6\frac{1}{2}$ miles an hour. Six hours later a second messenger followed and in $4\frac{7}{8}$ hours overtook the first just as he was entering the city. At what rate did the second messenger go? How far was it to Washington?

68. How far could a man ride at the rate of 8 miles an hour so as to walk back at the rate of 4 miles an hour and be gone only 9 hours?

69. Two persons start at 10 A.M. from towns A and B, $55\frac{1}{2}$ miles apart. The one starting from A walks at the rate of $4\frac{1}{4}$ miles an hour, but stops 2 hours on the way; the other walks at the rate of $3\frac{3}{4}$ miles an hour without stopping. When will they meet? How far will each have traveled?

Suggestion. Let x equal the number of hours.

70. A boy who runs at the rate of $12\frac{1}{2}$ yards per second, starts 16 yards behind another whose rate is 11 yards per second. How soon will the first boy be 8 yards ahead of the second?

71. A rectangle whose length is 4 ft. more than its width would have its area increased 56 sq. ft. if its length and width were each made 2 ft. more. What are its dimensions?

72. The length of a room is double its width. If the length were 3 ft. less and the width 3 ft. more, the area would be increased 27 sq. ft. Find the dimensions of the room.

73. A floor is two-thirds as wide as it is long. If the width were 2 ft. more and the length 4 ft. less, the area would be diminished 22 sq. ft. What are its dimensions?

74. A rectangle has its length and width respectively 4 ft. longer and 2 ft. shorter than the side of an equivalent square. Find its area.

75. An enclosed garden is 24 ft. greater in length than in width. 684 sq. ft. is used for a walk 3 ft. wide extending around the garden inside the fence. How long is the garden?

76. Factor $\dfrac{x^2}{4} - \dfrac{y^2z^4}{9m^6}$, $x^6 - 27y^3$, $a^{16} - b^{16}$, $2c - 4c^3 + 2c^5$.

77. Extract the square root of $12x^4 - 24x + 9 + x^6 - 22x^3 - 4x^5 + 28x^2$.

78. What must be subtracted from the sum of $4x^3 + 3x^2y - y^3$, $4x^2y - 3x^3$, $7x^2y + 9y^3 - 2x^2y$, to leave the remainder $2x^3 - 3x^2y + y^3$?

79. Find the G.C.F. of $x\,(x+1)^2$, $x^2(x^2-1)$, and $2x^3 - 2x^2 - 4x$.

80. From one end of a line I cut off 5 feet less than one-fifth of it, and from the other end 4 feet more than one-fourth of it, and then there remained 34 feet. How long was the line?

81. A can do twice as much work as B, B can do twice as much as C, and together they can complete a piece of work in 4 days. In what time can each alone complete the work.

82. Separate 57 into two parts, such that one divided by the other may give 5 as a quotient, with 3 as a remainder.

83. Divide 92 into two parts, such that one divided by the other may give 4 as a quotient, with 2 as a remainder.

84. Fourteen persons engaged a yacht, but before sailing, four of the company withdrew, by which the expense of each was increased $4. What was paid for the yacht?

85. Find two consecutive numbers such that a fifth of the larger shall equal the difference between a third and an eighth of the smaller.

86. A is 24 years older than B, and A's age is as much above 50 as B's is below 40. What is the age of each?

87. Find the number, whose double added to 16 will be as much above 70 as the number itself is below 60.

88. A hare takes 5 leaps to a dog's 4, but 3 of the dog's leaps are equal to 4 of the hare's; the hare has a start of 20 leaps. How many leaps will the hare take before he is caught?

    Suggestion. Let $5x$ equal the number of leaps the hare will take, and let m equal the length of one leap.

89. A greyhound takes 3 leaps to a hare's 5, but 2 of the greyhound's leaps are equal to 4 of the hare's. If the hare has a start of 48 leaps, how soon will the greyhound overtake him?

90. A hare has 40 leaps the start of a dog. When will he be caught if 5 of his leaps are equal to 4 of the dog's, and if he takes 7 leaps while the dog takes 6?

SIMULTANEOUS EQUATIONS.

48. ILLUS. $\left.\begin{array}{r} x+y=8,\ x=3 \\ 4x-y=7,\ y=5 \end{array}\right\}$ in both equations.

Simultaneous equations are equations in which the same unknown numbers have the same value.

One equation containing more than one unknown number cannot be solved. There must be as many simultaneous equations as there are unknown numbers.

$$\text{ILLUS. 1. Solve} \begin{cases} x + 3y = 17, \\ 2x + y = 9. \end{cases}$$

Multiply the first equation by 2;

$$\begin{array}{rc} \text{then} & 2x + 6y = 34, \\ \text{but} & \underline{2x + y = 9} \\ \text{Subtracting,} & 5y = 25 \\ & y = 5. \end{array}$$

To find the value of x, substitute the value of y in the second equation:

$$2x + 5 = 9, 2x = 4, x = 2.$$

$$Ans. \begin{cases} x = 2, \\ y = 5 \end{cases}$$

$$\text{ILLUS. 2. Solve} \begin{cases} 3x + 4y = 12, \\ 5x - 6y = 1. \end{cases}$$

Multiply the first equation by 3, and the second equation by 2,

$$\begin{array}{rrrl} & 9x & +12y = & 36 \\ & \underline{10x} & \underline{-12y =} & \underline{\ \ 2} \\ \text{Adding,} & 19x & & 38 \therefore x = 2. \end{array}$$

Substituting, $6 + 4y = 12$, $4y = 6$, $y = 1\frac{1}{2}$.

Multiply one or both of the equations by such a number that one of the unknown numbers shall have like coefficients. If the signs of the terms having like coefficients are alike, subtract one equation from the other; if unlike, add the equations.

Exercise 55.

Solve:

1. $\begin{cases} x + y = 4, \\ 3x - 2y = 7. \end{cases}$

2. $\begin{cases} x - y = 2, \\ 2x + 5y = 18. \end{cases}$

3. $\begin{cases} 5x + 2y = 47, \\ 2x - y = 8. \end{cases}$

4. $\begin{cases} 4x - 3y = 10, \\ 6x + 4y = 49. \end{cases}$

5. $\begin{cases} 8x - 2y = 6, \\ 10x + 7y = 36. \end{cases}$

6. $\begin{cases} 2x - 5y = -11, \\ 3x + y = 9. \end{cases}$

7. $\begin{cases} 7x - 3y = 41, \\ 2x + y = 12. \end{cases}$

8. $\begin{cases} 2x + 9y = -5, \\ 11x + 15y = 7. \end{cases}$

9. $\begin{cases} 4y - 2x = 4, \\ 10y + 3x = -8. \end{cases}$

10. $\begin{cases} 3x - 5y = 15, \\ 5x + 3y = 8. \end{cases}$

11. $\begin{cases} 3y - 2x = 3, \\ 4y - 6x = 2\frac{1}{3}. \end{cases}$

12. $\begin{cases} 3x + 2y = 11, \\ 7x - 5y = 190. \end{cases}$

13. $\begin{cases} \frac{1}{2}x + \frac{1}{3}y = 11, \\ 8x + \frac{2}{5}y = 102. \end{cases}$

14. $\begin{cases} 5x + 2y = 66, \\ \frac{x}{3} + \frac{3y}{4} = 15\frac{1}{2}. \end{cases}$

15. $\begin{cases} \frac{3x}{5} - \frac{2y}{7} = 35, \\ x + 2y = -63. \end{cases}$

16. $\begin{cases} x - \frac{3y}{5} = 6, \\ \frac{2x}{3} + 7y = 189. \end{cases}$

17. $\begin{cases} \frac{x+2y}{3x-y} = 1, \\ \frac{4y-x}{3+x-2y} = 2\frac{1}{2}. \end{cases}$

18. $\begin{cases} \frac{x+2y}{x-2} = -5\frac{2}{3}, \\ \frac{2y-4x}{3-y} = -6. \end{cases}$

19. $\begin{cases} y - \frac{2y+x}{3} = \frac{2x+y}{4} - 8\frac{3}{4}, \\ \frac{3x+y}{2} - \frac{y}{3} = \frac{109}{10} + \frac{4y-x}{5}. \end{cases}$

20. $\begin{cases} x + y = a, \\ x - y = b. \end{cases}$

21. $\begin{cases} \frac{3x-19}{2} + 4 = \frac{3y+x}{3} + \frac{5x-3}{2}, \\ \frac{4x+5y}{16} + \frac{2x+y}{2} = \frac{9x-7}{8} + \frac{3y+9}{4}. \end{cases}$

22. $\begin{cases} \frac{1}{5}(3x - 2y) + \frac{1}{3}(5x - 3y) = x, \\ \frac{4x-3y}{2} + \frac{2}{3}x - y = 1 + y. \end{cases}$

23. If 1 is added to the numerator of a fraction, its value is $\frac{1}{8}$; but if 4 is added to its denominator, its value is $\frac{1}{4}$. What is the fraction?

    Suggestion. Letting x equal the numerator, and y the denominator, form two equations.

24. If 2 is subtracted from both numerator and denominator of a certain fraction, its value is $\frac{3}{5}$; and if 1 is added to both numerator and denominator, its value is $\frac{2}{3}$. What is the fraction?

25. If 2 is added to both numerator and denominator of a certain fraction, its value is $\frac{2}{3}$; but if 3 is subtracted from both numerator and denominator, its value is $\frac{1}{2}$. What is the fraction?

26. If 3 be subtracted from the numerator of a certain fraction, and 3 be added to the denominator, its value will be $\frac{1}{2}$; but if 5 be added to the numerator, and 5 be subtracted from its denominator, its value will be 2. What is the fraction?

27. The sum of two numbers divided by 2 is 43, and their difference divided by 2 is 19. What are the numbers?

28. The sum of two numbers divided by 3 gives as a quotient 30, and their difference divided by 9 gives 4. What are the numbers?

29. Five years ago the age of a father was four times that of his son; five years hence the age of the father will be $2\frac{1}{3}$ times that of the son. What are their ages?

30. Seven years ago John was one-half as old as Henry, but five years hence he will be three-quarters as old. How old is each?

31. *A* and *B* own herds of cows. If *A* should sell 6 cows, and *B* should buy 6, they would have the same number; if *B* should sell 4 cows to *A*, he would have only half as many as A. How many cows are there in each herd?

32. The cost of 5 pounds of tea and 7 pounds of coffee is \$4.94; the cost of 3 pounds of tea and 6 pounds of coffee is \$3.54. What is the cost of the tea and coffee per pound?

33. What is the price of corn and oats when 4 bushels of corn with 6 bushels of oats cost \$4.66, and 5 bushels of corn with 9 bushels of oats cost \$6.38?

34. A merchant mixes tea which cost him 87 cents a pound with tea which cost him 29 cents a pound. The cost of the mixture is $17.98. He sells the mixture at 55 cents a pound and gains $2.92. How many pounds of each did he put into the mixture?

QUADRATIC EQUATIONS.

49. ILLUS. 1. $ax^2 = b$, $7x^2 - 10 = 5 + 2x^3$.
ILLUS. 2. $x^2 + 8x = 20$, $ax^2 + bx - c = bx^2 + d$.

A **quadratic equation** is an equation in which, the highest power of the unknown number is a square. It is called an equation of the second degree.

If it contains only the second power of the unknown number (Illus. 1), it is called a **pure quadratic equation**. If it contains both the first and second powers of the unknown number (Illus. 2), it is called an **affected quadratic equation**.

50. ILLUS. Solve $x^2 - \frac{x^2-10}{3} = 35 - \frac{x^2+50}{5}$.

$$15x^2 - 5x^2 + 50 = 525 - 3x^2 - 150. \quad (1)$$

$$13x^2 = 325. \quad (2)$$

$$x^2 = 25. \quad (3)$$

$$x = \pm 5. \quad (4)$$

To solve a pure quadratic equation, reduce to the form $x^2 = a$ and take the square root of each member.

Exercise 56

Solve:

1. $5x^2 - 12 = 33$.

2. $3x^2 + 4 = 16$.

3. $4x^2 + ll = 136 - x^2$.

4. $5(3x^2 - 1) = 11(x^2 + 1)$.

5. $\dfrac{2}{5x^2} - \dfrac{1}{3x^2} = \dfrac{4}{15}$.

6. $\dfrac{x^2 - 1}{6} + \dfrac{1}{4} = \dfrac{x^2 + 1}{8}$.

7. $(x + 3)^2 = 6x + 58$.

8. $6x + 2 + \dfrac{16}{x} = \dfrac{15 + 40x}{4} - 1\dfrac{3}{4}$.

9. $\frac{x-3}{x-1}+\frac{x+1}{x+3}+\frac{8}{x^2+2x-3}=0.$

10. $\frac{x+1}{x-1}+\frac{2(x-3)}{x-2}=\frac{16-9x}{x^2-3x+2}.$

11. $\frac{1}{(2-x)(3-x)}-\frac{2}{(1-x)(x-3)}+\frac{1}{(x-1)(x-2)}=\frac{1}{2-x}+\frac{1}{(x-1)(2-x)(x-3)}$

12. $\frac{1}{6x+6}-\frac{1}{2x+2}+\frac{10}{3-3x^2}=\frac{x}{3(1-x)}.$

13. A father is 30 years old, and his son is two years old. In how many years will the father be three times as old as his son?

14. Divide the number 112 into two parts such that the smaller divided by their difference will give as a quotient 3.

15. The numerator of a fraction is 4 less than the denominator; if 30 be added to the denominator, or if 10 be subtracted from the numerator, the resulting fractions will be equal. What is the original fraction?

51. ILLUS. Solve $\frac{x-1}{x-2}-\frac{x-3}{x-4}=-\frac{2}{3}.$

$$3x^2-15x+12-3x^2+15x-18=-2x^2+12x-16.$$
$$2x^2-12x=-10.$$
$$x^2-6x=-5.$$
$$x^2-6x-5=0.$$
$$(x-5)(x-1)=0.$$

This equation will be satisfied if either factor is equal to zero. Placing each factor in turn equal to zero, and solving,

x-5 = 0, x-1 = 0,
x = 5; x = 1.

Ans. $x=5$ or 1.

To solve an affected quadratic equation, reduce the equation to the form $x^2+bx+c=O$, factor the first member, place each factor in turn equal to zero, and solve the simple equations thus formed.

Exercise 57.

Solve:

1. $x^2+3x=18.$

2. $x^2+5x=14.$

3. $x(x-1)=72.$

4. $x^2=10x-21.$

5. $23x=120+x^2.$

6. $187=x^2+6x.$

7. $x^2-2bx=-b^2.$

8. $x^2=4ax-3a^2.$

9. $x^2+(a-1)x=a.$

10. $adx-acx^2=bcx-bd.$

11. $(x+3)(x-3)=8(x+3).$

12. $(x+2)(x-5)=4(x-4).$

13. $\frac{x}{5}+\frac{2}{x}=1\frac{2}{5}.$

14. $\frac{x}{3}-2=\frac{x^2}{12}-\frac{x}{2}.$

15. $\frac{8}{x-2}-3+\frac{x+1}{7}=0.$

16. $\frac{x}{x+1}-2\frac{1}{6}+\frac{x+1}{x}=0.$

17. $x+4=3x-\frac{24}{x-1}.$

18. $\frac{x-1}{x+1}+\frac{x+3}{x-3}=\frac{2(x+2)}{x-2}.$

19. $\frac{x-1}{x+2}-\frac{3x^2+2}{x^2-4}=\frac{3x}{2-x}.$

20. $\frac{2x}{3-x}+\frac{2x(x-3)}{x^2-9}=\frac{x-3}{x+3}.$

21. At what time between 4 and 5 o'clock are the hands of a clock opposite each other?

22. John, having three times as much money as Lewis, gave Lewis \$2, and then had twice as much as Lewis. How much had each at first?

23. A fish is 3 feet long; its head is equal in length to the tail, and its body is five times the length of the head and tail together. What is the length of the head?

24. In how many days can A, B, and C build a boat if they work together, provided A alone can build it in 24 days, B in 18 days, and C in 30 days?

The above method of solving affected quadratic equations is the simplest of three methods commonly used, and will not solve all possible cases; the method given for solving simultaneous equations is only one of three known methods; the cases in factoring are less than half of those usually taken. In fact, we have made only a beginning in the subject of algebra; much more lies ahead along the lines which we have been following. *Can you grasp more clearly the conditions given in any problem presented to you, and see more definitely just what is required, than when you began this study? Do you possess greater ability to think out problems? Has the use of letters to represent numbers made you think more exactly what is to be done, and what the operations mean?* If so, your knowledge of numbers is broader, and you already know that

Algebra is the knowledge which has for its object general truths about numbers.

Exercise 58. (General Review.)

1. When $a = l$, $b = 3$, $c = 5$, and $d = O$, what is the value of
$$\frac{4a + b^2 + b^2c^2 + ad}{b^2 + c^2 + d^2} - \frac{1 + a^2c^2}{a^2 + c^2 + d^2} + \frac{a^2 + b^2 + d^2}{1 + a^2b^2 + bd} - \frac{a^2 + 2ab + b^2}{b^2 - 2bc + c^2}?$$

2. Prove that $(x^2 + xy + y^2)(x^2 - xy + y^2) = \dfrac{x^6 - y^6}{x^2 - y^2}$

3. Solve $(x + 5)^2 - (x + 1)^2 - 16x = (x - 1)^2 - (x - 5)^2$.

4. A tank is filled by two pipes, A and B, running together, in 12 hours, and by the pipe B alone in 20 hours. In what time will the pipe A alone fill it?

5. Find the G.C.F. of $x^3 + 1 - x - x^2$, $x^3 + x - 1 - x^2$, $x^4 - 1$, and $x^2 - 4x + 3$.

6. Divide $a^5 + a^4b - a^3b^2 + a^3 - 2ab^2 + b^3$ by $a^3 - b + a$.

7. Find the square root of $5y^4 + 1 + 12y^5 - 2y - 2y^3 + 4y^6 + 7y^2$.

8. Expand
$$(x + 1)(x + 2) - (2x + 1)(2x + 3) + (x - 4)(x - 9) + (x - 5)^2.$$

9. Solve $\dfrac{x + 2}{x - 2} + \dfrac{x - 2}{x + 2} = \dfrac{5}{2}$.

10. Simplify
$$\left(\frac{1}{x - 1} - \frac{3}{(x + 3)(x - 1)}\right) \div \left(\frac{1}{x + 3} + \frac{1}{(x - 1)(x + 3)}\right).$$

II.

11. Add $2(a-c)^3 - 10x^3y - 7(a-c)$, $6(a-c) - 2(a-c)^3 - 10x^3y$, $3(a-c) - (a-c)^3 + 2x^3y$, $2(a-c) + x^3y - (a-c)^3$, $4(a-c) + 5(a-c)^3 + 2x^3y$, $3(a-c) - 2x^3y - 6(a-c)^3$.

12. Solve $bx - b^2 = 3b^2 - 4bx$.

13. Factor $x^6 + 2x^3 - 3$, $ax^2 - ay^2 + by^2 - bx^2$, $27x^3 + (y+z)^3$.

14. Find the fraction which becomes equal to one when six is added to the numerator, and equal to one-third when four is added to the denominator.

15. Simplify $\dfrac{\frac{a^2}{b^3} + \frac{1}{a}}{\frac{a}{b^3} - \frac{1}{b} + \frac{1}{ab}}$.

16. Solve $\dfrac{7x+9}{4} = \left(x - \dfrac{2x-1}{9}\right) + 7$.

17. Six years ago John was five times as old as Sarah. If he is twice as old as Sarah now, what are their ages?

18. Multiply together $\frac{1-x^2}{1+y}$, $\frac{1-y^2}{x+x^2}$, and $1 + \frac{x}{1-x}$.

19. Simplify $a^2 - (b^2 - c^2) - \{b^2 - (c^2 - a^2)\} + \{c^2 - (b^2 - a^2)\}$.

20. x times y is how many times a?

III.

21. Add $2x + y - 2a + 55\frac{1}{2}b$, $24b - y + 2x + a$, $3a - 2y - 4x - 81b$, and subtract the result from $2y + 3a + \frac{1}{2}b + 3x$.

22. Divide $\frac{11}{8}a^2 - \frac{5}{4}a^3 - \frac{1}{2}a + a^4$ by $a^2 - \frac{1}{2}a$.

23. A can do a piece of work in 3 days which B can do in 5 days. In what time can they do it working together?

24. Simplify $\dfrac{a-b}{a^2 - ab + b^2} + \dfrac{ab}{a^3 + b^3} + \dfrac{1}{a+b}$.

25. Factor $x^2 - 9x - 52$, $1 - a^{16}$, $(a^2 + b^2)^2 + 2(a^4 - b^4) + (a^2 - b^2)^2$.

26. Solve $\dfrac{3x}{4} - \dfrac{x-10}{2} = x - 6 - \dfrac{x-4}{2}$.

27. The sum of the ages of a man and his son is 100 years; one-tenth of the product of their ages exceeds the father's age by 180. How old are they?

28. Solve $x = 9 - \frac{y}{2}$, $y = 11 + \frac{x}{3}$.

29. From what must $3x^4 - 2x^3 + x - 6$ be subtracted to produce unity?

30. Find the following roots: $\sqrt{5.5225}$, $\sqrt[3]{32.768}$.

IV.

31. Find the value of $\frac{4x^3+2y^3}{ab}+\frac{2y^3+4z^3}{z^3+y^2}-\frac{b^3-z^2b}{a^2b}$, if $x=1$, $y=2$, $z=0$, $a=4$, and $b=5$.

32. Solve $\frac{4}{x-6}-\frac{3}{x-9}=\frac{1}{x-3}$.

33. Find three consecutive numbers whose sum is 78.

34. Find the G.C.F. of $2a^3-12a-2a^2$, a^4-4a^2 and $4a^3b+16ab+16a^2b$.

35. Divide $\frac{x^4-y^4}{x^2-2xy+y^2}$ by $\frac{x^2+xy}{x-y}$.

36. A fraction becomes $\frac{3}{4}$ by the addition of three to the numerator and one to the denominator. If one is subtracted from the numerator and three from the denominator, it becomes $\frac{1}{2}$. What is the fraction?

37. Expand $\left(\frac{3a^2b(m+n)^2}{4xy^3}(a-b)^3\right)^3$, $\sqrt{\frac{50x^4(a+b)^7}{32y^6z^2(a+b)}}$.

38. If a certain number is multiplied by itself, the result is $9x^4-4x+10x^2+1-12x^3$. Find the number.

39. Simplify $\frac{ax-x^2}{(a+x)^2}\times\frac{a^2+ax}{(a-x)^2}\div\frac{2ax}{a^2-x^2}$.

40. Solve $18x-20y=3$, $\frac{4y-2}{3}-\frac{5x}{2}=0$.

V.

41. Factor x^4+5x^2+6, $x^2-14x+49$, $x^2-(y+z)^2$.

42. Add $xy-\frac{9}{8}x-\frac{7}{12}(x^2-y^2)-5x^2y^2$, $\frac{5}{8}x-xy+9x^2y^2+\frac{2}{3}(x^2-y^2)$, $\frac{1}{9}x^2y^2-xy+\frac{1}{4}x+\frac{3}{4}(x^2-y^2)$, $2xy+\frac{1}{4}x-\frac{5}{6}(x^2-y^2)-4x^2y^2$.

43. At what times between 7 and 8 o'clock are the hands of a clock six minutes apart?

44. Simplify $\frac{x^2-5x+6}{x^2-2x+1}\times\frac{x^2-4x+3}{x^2-4x+4}\div\frac{x^2-6x+9}{x^2-3x+2}$.

45. Solve $\frac{x+2}{b+2}=2-\frac{x+1}{b+1}$.

46. Factor $\frac{x^6}{y^6}-\frac{a^2b^4}{c^2}$, $\frac{x^2}{y^2}-\frac{5x}{y}-14$, $\frac{x^2}{y^2}-2+\frac{y^2}{x^2}$.

47. A, who works only two-thirds as fast as B, can build a stone wall in 12 days. In what time could A and B together build the wall?

48. Solve $\dfrac{x+y}{2} - \dfrac{x-y}{3} = 8$, $\frac{x+y}{3} + \frac{x-y}{4} = 11$.

49. Expand $(1+2x)^3$, $(2x^2 - 3a^2b^3)^4$.

50. Reduce $\dfrac{(a^4+2a^2b^2+b^4)(a^4+b^4)}{a^8-b^8}$ to lowest terms.

VI.

51. y is how much greater than x?

52. Subtract $3x^3+4x^2y-7xy^2+10y^3$ from $4x^3-2x^2y+4xy^2+4y^3$ and find the value of the remainder when $x=2$ and $y=1$.

53. The length and width of a rectangle are respectively 5 feet longer and 4 feet.shorter than the side of an equivalent square. What is its area?

54. Find the L.C.M. of a^2-3-2a, a^2-1, and $2a^2-6a+4$.

55. Simplify $\dfrac{\frac{b}{4a} - 1 + \frac{a}{b}}{\frac{b}{2a} - \frac{2a}{b}}$.

56. Solve $\dfrac{x-1}{3} + \dfrac{3}{x-1} = 2$.

57. Factor $a^4b + 8ac^3bm^6$, $4c^3x^2 + cy^2 + 4c^2xy$, $x^6 - 1$.

58. Multiply $1 - \dfrac{1}{2}x - \dfrac{1}{3}x^2 + \dfrac{1}{4}x^3$ by $1 - \frac{1}{3}x^2 - \frac{1}{4}x^3 - \frac{1}{2}x$.

59. Find the cube root of $6x^4 + 7x^3 + 3x^5 + 6x^2 + x^6 + 1 + 3x$.

60. Divide $12x^2y^2 - 4y^4 - 6x^3y + x^4$ by $x^2 + 2y^2 - 3xy$.

VII.

61. Add $\frac{1}{10}a^3 - \frac{4}{5}a^4 - \frac{1}{5}a^2 + \frac{3}{10}a$, $\frac{1}{4}a^2 - \frac{4}{5}a - \frac{5}{7}a^4 - \frac{1}{8}a^3$, $\frac{5}{7}a^4 + \frac{1}{8}a^3 + \frac{3}{4}a^2 + \frac{2}{5}a$, $\frac{4}{5}a^4 + \frac{1}{5}a^2 + \frac{2}{5}a^3 + \frac{1}{10}a$.

62. Solve $x(a-x) + x(b-x) = 2(x-a)(b-x)$.

63. Factor $x^4 - 22x^2 - 75$, $16 - x^8$, $(a+b)^2 - (a-b)^2$.

64. A piece of work can be finished by 3 men in 8 days, or by 5 women in 6 days, or by 6 boys in 6 days. In what time can 2 men, 3 women, and 3 boys do the work?

65. Solve $\dfrac{3x+19}{2} - \left(\dfrac{x+1}{6} + 3\right) = \dfrac{5x+2}{3} - \left(3 - \dfrac{3x-1}{2}\right)$.

66. Expand $\left(\frac{a}{b}-\frac{c}{d}\right)^3$, $\left(\frac{c}{d}+1\right)\left(\frac{c^2}{d^2}-\frac{c}{d}+1\right)$.

67. What number is that, the sum of whose third and fourth parts is less by two than the square of its sixth part?

68. Solve $\dfrac{x}{5}-\dfrac{y}{7}=1$, $\frac{2x}{3}-\frac{y}{2}=3$.

69. Divide m by $1+y$ to four terms.

70. If x is $\frac{3}{5}$ of a number, what is the number?

VIII.

71. The head of a fish is 6 inches long, the tail is as long as the head and half the body, and the body is as long as the head and tail. What is the length of the fish?

72. Add $4a-5x-15y$, $a+18x+8y$, $4a-7x+11y$, $a+3x+5y$, and multiply the result by the difference between $11a+7y$ and $10a+6y-x$.

73. Divide $2x^2+\frac{9}{2}x^4+\frac{8}{9}$ by $2x+3x^2+\frac{4}{3}$.

74. How many numbers each equal to $1-2x+x^2$ must be added together to equal $5x^6-6x^5+1$?

75. Factor $a^3+5a^2-4a-20$, x^6-y^6, $2x^5-8x^3y^2+6xy^4$.

76. A courier who travels at the rate of 5 miles an hour is followed, 4 hours later, by another who travels at the rate of 15 miles in 2 hours. In how many hours will the second overtake the first?

77. Divide $\dfrac{1}{1-x}-\dfrac{1}{1+x}$ by $\dfrac{1}{1-x}+\dfrac{1}{1+x}$.

78. Solve $3x-4y=-6$, $10x+2y=26$.

79. $3xy-3a^2+4b^2-5cd+4xy-6a^2-7b^2+7cd+3xy-6a^2+6b^2-3cd-5xy+7a^2-6b^2+4cd+4xy+7a^2-7b^2+4cd-6xy-6a^2+3b^2-7cd+7a^2=?$

80. Simplify $3x-5-\{2(4-x)-3(x-2)\}+\{3-(5+2x)-2\}$.

ANSWERS TO A FIRST BOOK IN ALGEBRA.

Exercise 1.

1. 43; 86.
2. Carriage, \$375; horse, \$125.
3. C, \$31; J, \$155.
4. 8; 56.
5. 8 miles.
6. Needles, 8; thread, 64.
7. 224 girls; 448 boys.
8. 25; 275.
9. H, 6 qts.; J, 18 qts.
10. Lot, \$720; house, \$3600.
11. Mr. A, 72; son, 24.
12. 50 A.; 300 A.
13. Dict., \$7.20; rhet, \$.90.
14. 112; 4144.
15. Aleck, 56; Arthur, 8.
16. Mother, 28; daughter, 4.
17. J, 15 yrs.; M, 5 yrs.

Exercise 2.

1. Necktie, \$.75; hat, \$3; boots, \$3.75.
2. 30; 45; 15 miles.
3. James, 15; sister, 5; brother, 10.
4. Pig, \$10; cow, \$30; horse, \$50.
5. A, 35; B, 15; C, 5.
6. 12; 48.
7. 8 men; 40 women.
8. Henry, \$200; John, \$400; James, \$800.
9. 4500 ft.; 13,500 ft.; 27,000 ft.
10. 15; 45; 60 pigeons.
11. 165; 33; 11.
12. A, \$44; B, \$11; C, \$55.
13. Calf, \$8; cow, \$16; horse, \$48.
14. 150; 450 gal.
15. Cow, \$30; lamb, \$5.
16. Tea, 90; coffee, 30.
17. Mrs. C, \$25,000; Henry, \$5000.

Exercise 3.

1. 14 boys; 21 girls.
2. 14 yrs.; 29 yrs.
3. 492; 587 votes.
4. 22; 48.
5. J, 79; H, 64.
6. Flour, 27 bbls.; meal, 30 bbls.
7. 23 Hol.; 40 Jer.
8. \$18; \$26.
9. 40; 59.

10. 16; 19; 21.

11. 21; 17; 24.

12. $10,000; $11,500; $12,700.

13. 21; 38; 6.

14. 51; 28; 16 sheep.

15. A, 253; B, 350; C, 470 votes.

16. 17; 12; 24 A.

17. 36; 20; 55.

18. $50,000; $44,000; $24,000.

Exercise 4.

1. C, 34; H, 15.
2. 26 pear; 7 apple.
3. J, 16 qts.; M, 7 qts.
4. 65.
5. 18.
6. 24.
7. 11.
8. Tea, $8.76; coffee, $1.63.
9. 15; 33 rooms.
10. 5; 6; 12.
11. 17; 20; 100.
12. $5000; $3000; $10,000.
13. $50; $68; $204.
14. A, $5000; B, $10,500; C, $31,500.
15. 8000; 24,250; 48,500ft.
16. Daughter, $25,000; son, $40,000; widow, $160,000.
17. Father, 14 qts.; older son, 7 qts.; younger son, 4 qts.
18. H, 200 stamps; J, 185 stamps; T, 189 stamps.

Exercise 5.

1. Blue, 5 yds.; white, 15 yds.
2. 3.
3. Walked 2 hrs.; rode 8 hrs.
4. Book, \$2; lamp, \$4.
5. 12.
6. 12 twos; 24 fives.
7. Tea, 67; coffee, 32.
8. Crackers,18 gingersnaps, 25
9. Lamp, \$1; vase, \$1.50.
10. House, \$4500; barn, \$3300.
11. 12,000; 13,500 ft.
12. 29 gal.; 24 gal.
13. Johnson, \$6000; May, \$1500.
14. 27; 10; 42.
15. 3; 17; 51.
16. 3 bbls.; 9 boxes.
17. 18; 90; 180.
18. 84; 132.

Exercise 6.

1. 4.
2. 7.
3. 12 yrs.
4. \$6.25.
5. \$8.
6. 8 sheep.
7. 121; 605.
8. 142; 994.

9. $500; $1450; $2900.
10. W, 6 yrs.; J, 9 yrs.
11. 25; 15 marbles.
12. 16.
13. Oranges, 35 cents; apples, 20 cents.
14. 9; 15.
15. 30 yrs.; 32 yrs.
16. Cow, $30; horse,$45.
17. 5.
18. Boots, $5; clothes, $18.

Exercise 7.

1. 14 yrs.; 56 yrs.
2. Corn, 60; wheat, 300.
3. $3000; $9000.
4. 70 miles; 35 miles.
5. 45; 720.
6. 189.
7. J, 3 yrs.; M, 15 yrs.
8. 96.
9. $40,000.
10. 24 marbles.
11. $30,000.
12. 300 oranges.
13. 90.
14. 60,000ft.
15. 70ft.
16. 72 sq. rds.
17. A, $22,500; B, $7500.
18. 30.

Exercise 8.

1. 4.
2. 45 marbles.
3. 12; 24; 6 cows.
4. 16.
5. 45.
6. 6048.
7. $3000.
8. 24.
9. 14.
10. 48,000 ft.
11. 30.
12. 18; 9; 63.
13. 56; 21; 7.
14. 16; 4; 56; 36.
15. Coffee, 18 lbs.; tea, 20 lbs.; cocoa, 24 lbs.
16. $2500; $5000; $7500.
17. J, 9 cents; P, 81 cents.
18. $12,000.

Exercise 9.

1. 35; 21.
2. 24; 18.
3. 42; 30 miles.
4. 30; 54 yrs.
5. J, 10 boxes; H, 16 boxes.
6. 33 tons; $27\frac{1}{2}$ tons.
7. John, 28yrs.; James, 32yrs.
8. $1000; $625.

9. 240 girls; 180 boys.

10. 150 lemons.

11. 21,000 ft.; 6000 ft.

12. 20; 12; 10; 10 miles.

13. 126 cu. yds.

14. M, 390; H, 130.

15. 39; 41; 32; 27.

16. 3205; 2591; 1309.

17. 20 miles; 4 miles; 48 miles.

Exercise 10.

1. $x + 9$.

2. $a + p$.

3. $8b$.

4. $x + y$.

5. $c + 5$.

6. dx.

7. $m + l + v + c$ dols.

8. $x + y + z$ yrs.

9. bm.

10. $d + 1$.

11. $y + z + s$ cts.

12. $m + 1$.

13. yx.

14. $x + 40 + a$.

15. 28; 46.

Exercise 11.

1. $a - b$ or $b - a$.
2. $b - 10$.
3. $a + b - c$.
4. $a - 2$, $a - 1$, a, $a + 1$, $a + 2$.
5. $a - b$ dols.
6. $c - 8$.
7. $x - 3$, $x - 6$, $x - 9$.
8. $c - b$ dols.
9. $x - 5$.
10. x, $x + 9$, or x, $x - 9$.
11. $x - 75$ dols.
12. $m + x$ dols.
13. $c - f$ cts.
14. $b - e$ dols.
15. $l + 4 + m - x$ dols.
16. $c - a - b$.
17. $429; 636$ votes.
18. $m + x - y + b - z$ dols.
19. $80 - c$ dols.
20. $x, 60 - x$.

Exercise 12.

1. $2x$.
2. xyz.
3. $100x$ cts.
4. abc.
5. ad cts.
6. mb miles.

7. ax hills.

8. x^3.

9. a^9.

10. d^a.

11. $3m^3 + a^2$.

12. $x^{2m} + x^m$.

13. $\frac{6}{100}mx$ dols., or $6mx$ cts.

14. $3c - 8$ boys; $4c - 8$ boys and girls.

15. $9x$ days.

16. $3x$ thirds.

17. $5b$ fifths.

18. $m - x + 2a$ dols.

19. $12a - 39$.

Exercise 13.

1. $\frac{5a}{3c}$.

2. $\frac{y}{100}$ dols.

3. $\frac{x}{a}$ books.

4. $\frac{m}{y}$ days.

5. $\frac{x}{b}$ dols.

6. $\frac{a+b}{c}$.

7. $a + \frac{b}{c}$.

8. $a + \frac{a}{2}$, or $\frac{3}{2}a$.

9. $300x$.

10. $18b - 3x$ dols.

11. A, $\dfrac{1}{x}$; B, $\dfrac{1}{y}$; C, $\dfrac{1}{z}$; all, $\dfrac{1}{x} + \dfrac{1}{y} + \dfrac{1}{z}$.

12. a^2 sq. ft.

13. $100a + 10b + 25c$ cts.

14. $\dfrac{x}{y}$.

15. $\dfrac{n}{m}$ chestnuts.

16. 12; 18 apples.

Exercise 14.

10. 11.

11. 7.

12. 21.

13. 78.

14. 46.

15. -74.

16. $-1\frac{1}{3}$.

17. $-4\frac{1}{4}$.

18. 5.

19. 6 apples; 12 pears.

20. 36 years.

Exercise 15.

1. $24x$.

2. $25ab$.

3. $-18ax^3$.

4. $-42x$.

5. $10a^2$.

6. $-10abc^2$.

7. $6ab - x^2$.

8. $10ax - 4bc$.

9. $-16a^2$.

10. $8a^4b + 3ab - x^5$.

11. $\frac{3}{2}a$.

12. $-\frac{7}{12}b$.

13. $m + d + c - x$ cts.

14. $a - x - 5 + y$ miles.

15. $5a + 4b + 5c$.

16. $x + y - z$.

17. $-3z - a$.

18. $2x^3 + 4x^2 - 2x + 17$.

19. $a^3 + b^3 + c^3$.

20. $2a^m + 1$.

21. $2a^2b^2c$.

22. $23x^3 - 20x^2 + 27x + 6$.

23. $x^5y + 12x^4y^2 - 16x^3y^3 - 8xy^5$.

24. $5x + 3y + z - a - 3b$.

25. $a^3 + b^3 + c^3 - 3abc$.

26. $mb + c$ men.

27. $x - 10$ cows; $z + 19$ horses.

28. 22 girls; 30 boys.

Exercise 16.

1. $2a^3$.
2. $12a^2b$.
3. $-9xy^3$.
4. $4x^my$.
5. $8x^2 - 3ax$.
6. $5xy + 7by$.
7. $2a^m$.
8. $9ax$.
9. $-3a - b + 14c$.
10. $4x - y + 2z$.

11. $8x^4 - 2x^3 + 4x^2 - 15x + 14.$

12. $20a^2b^2 + 16a^2b.$

13. $4x^3 - 2.$

14. $2x^m - x^{2m} - x^{3m}$

15. $2a^{2n} - 18a^nx^n - 9x^{2n}.$

16. $\frac{4}{3}a^2 - \frac{7}{2}a - \frac{1}{2}.$

17. $-2x^4y - 3x^3y^2 + 5xy^4 - y^5.$

18. $x - y + a.$

19. $-3a^2.$

20. $8x^3 - 2x.$

21. $27y^3 - 3z^3 - 6x^3 + 4yz^2 - 11z^2x.$

22. $4x^2 - 16x + 64.$

23. $-4a^2 + 6b^2 - 8bc + 6ab.$

24. $2x^4 - 3x^2 + 2x - 4.$

25. $5a^3 + 2a + 2.$

26. $-11a^2b + 4ab^2 - 12a^2b^2 - b^3.$

27. $b - a.$

28. $x - 3.$

29. $40 - y$ yrs.

30. $\frac{23}{a}$ hrs.

Exercise 17.

1. $2x + a + b + c - d.$

2. $a + c.$

3. $2a^2b - a^3 - 2b^3 - ab^2.$

4. $3xy - x^2 - 3y^2.$

5. $4b - 4c.$

6. $-2y.$

7. $-6b + 4c.$

8. $-b$.

17. $5(x-y)$.

18. $150-7(x+y)$.

19. $x+8$ yrs.

20. $3(x-35)$ dols.

Exercise 18.

1. $35cx$.

2. $-51acxy$.

3. $21ax^4y^3$.

4. $10a^3b^3c^4$.

5. $18acx^3y^3$.

6. $30a^3b^2c^4$.

7. $-x^3y^3z^3$.

8. $-a^4b^5c^2$.

9. $-\frac{2}{9}a^2cx^6y^4$.

10. $-\frac{3}{20}a^3b^5c^4$.

11. $\frac{100}{ab}$.

12. $100x$.

13. $100a+10b+c$.

14. $x+7$ or $x-7$.

Exercise 19.

1. $x^4y^2+x^3y^3+x^2y^4$.

2. $a^4b-a^3b^2+a^2b^3$.

3. $-2a^4b+6a^3b^2-2ab^4$.

4. $24x^4y^2+108x^3y^3+81xy^5$.

5. $a^5b^2-\frac{6}{25}a^4b^3-\frac{2}{5}a^3b^4$.

6. x^3+y^3.

7. $x^5 - 4x^4 + 5x^3 - 3x^2 + 2x - 1$.
8. $x^5 + x^4 - 4x^3 + x^2 + x$.
9. $x^2y^2 - 2xy^2n + y^2n^2 - m^2n^2 + 2xm^2n - x^2m^2$.
10. $x^7 + x^6 + 2x^5 + x^2 + x + 2$.
11. $a^6 + b^6$.
12. $x^3 - 3xyz + y^3 + z^3$.
13. $x^7 - y^7$.
14. $x^8 - 8x^4a^4 + 16a^8$.
15. $a^6 + 2a^3y^3 - 9a^4y^4 + y^6$.
16. $x^6 + x^5 + 2x^4 - 11x^3 - 17x^2 - 34x - 12$.
17. $6x^6 - 17x^5 - 12x^4 - 14x^3 + x^2 + 12x + 4$.
18. $5(x + y)$; $4(x - y)$.
19. $\frac{12}{35}$ of the field.
20. $\frac{1}{a} + \frac{1}{b}$.

Exercise 20.

1. $x^2 + 9x + 14$.
2. $x^2 + 7x + 6$.
3. $x^2 - 7x + 12$.
4. $x^2 - 7x + 10$.
5. $x^2 + 3x - 10$.
6. $x^2 + 4x - 21$.
7. $x^2 - x - 42$.
8. $x^2 - x - 30$.
9. $x^2 - 13x + 22$.
10. $x^2 - 14x + 13$.
11. $y^2 - 2y - 63$.
12. $x^2 + 20x + 51$.
13. $y^2 - 13y - 30$.

14. $y^2 + 18y + 32$.

15. $a^4 + 2a^2 - 35$.

16. $a^2 - 81$.

17. $m^4 - 18m^2 + 32$.

18. $b^6 + 2b^3 - 120$.

19. $x^2 - \frac{3}{4}x + \frac{1}{8}$.

20. $y^2 + \frac{1}{2}y + \frac{1}{18}$.

21. $m^2 + \frac{1}{3}m - \frac{2}{9}$.

22. $a^2 + \frac{1}{5}a - \frac{6}{25}$.

23. $x^2 - \frac{7}{6}x + \frac{1}{3}$.

24. $y^2 + \frac{19}{20}y + \frac{3}{20}$.

25. $21 - 10x + x^2$.

26. $15 - 8x + x^2$.

27. $42 - x - x^2$.

28. $33 + 8x - x^2$.

29. $x^2 - 9$.

30. $y^2 - 25$.

31. 21.

32. 12 cows.

Exercise 21.

1. a^4b^2.
2. x^3y^6.
3. a^8b^2.
4. $-x^9y^6$.
5. $27a^6y^3$.
6. $49a^2b^4c^6$.
7. $x^5y^5z^{10}$.
8. $m^8n^4d^4$.

9. $-125x^9y^{12}z^3$.

10. $121c^{10}d^{24}x^8$.

11. $\frac{1}{4}x^4a^2m^6$.

12. $\frac{1}{9}a^2b^6c^2$.

13. $225c^{12}d^2x^4$.

14. $-729x^3y^{15}z^6$.

15. $a^{36}b^8c^{16}d^8$.

16. $-x^{40}y^5z^{15}m^{10}n^5$.

17. $\frac{4}{9}a^4b^2c^8$.

18. $\frac{25}{36}m^2n^4x^6$.

19. $8b$ days.

20. $10a$ mills; $\frac{a}{100}$ dols.

Exercise 22.

1. $z^3 + 3z^2x + 3zx^2 + x^3$.

2. $a^4 + 4a^3y + 6a^2y^2 + 4ay^3 + y^4$.

3. $x^4 - 4x^3a + 6x^2a^2 - 4xa^3 + a^4$.

4. $a^3 - 3a^2m + 3am^2 - m^3$.

5. $m^2 + 2am + a^2$.

6. $x^2 - 2xy + y^2$.

7. $x^6 + 3x^4y^2 + 3x^2y^4 + y^6$.

8. $m^6 - 2m^3y^2 + y^4$.

9. $c^8 - 4c^6d^2 + 6c^4d^4 - 4c^2d^6 + d^8$.

10. $y^6 + 3y^4z^4 + 3y^2z^8 + z^{12}$.

11. $x^4y^2 + 2x^2yz + z^2$.

12. $a^8b^4 - 4a^6b^3c + 6a^4b^2c^2 - 4a^2bc^3 + c^4$.

13. $a^6 - 3a^4b^3c + 3a^2b^6c^2 - b^9c^3$.

14. $x^4y^2 - 2x^2ymn^3 + m^2n^6$.

15. $x^3 + 3x^2 + 3x + 1$.

16. $m^2 - 2m + 1$.

17. $b^8 - 4b^6 + 6b^4 - 4b^2 + 1$.

18. $y^9 + 3y^6 + 3y^3 + 1$.

19. $a^2b^2 - 4ab + 4$.

20. $x^4y^2 - 6x^2y + 9$.

21. $1 - 4x + 6x^2 - 4x^3 + x^4$.

22. $1 - 3y^2 + 3y^4 - y^6$.

23. $4x^2 + 12xy^2 + 9y^4$.

24. $27a^3b^3 - 27a^2b^2x^2y + 9abx^4y^2 - x^6y^3$.

25. $256m^4n^{12} - 768m^3n^9a^2b + 864m^2n^6a^4b^2 - 432mn^3a^6b^3 + 81a^8b^4$.

26. $\frac{1}{4}x^2 - xy + y^2$.

27. $1 - x^2 + \frac{1}{3}x^4 - \frac{1}{27}x^6$.

28. $x^8 - 12x^6 + 54x^4 - 108x^2 + 81$.

29. $20a^2 - d$ horses.

30. $100x - a^2$ cts.

31. $a(25 - x)$ cts.

32. 3.

33. −228.

Exercise 23.

1. $14x - 7$.
2. $b^8 - 2b^4 + 1$.
3. $10x^2 + 7y^2$.
4. \$160; \$80; \$60.
5. 13; 21.
6. $2a^3 + 4a^2 + 10$.
7. $\frac{1}{3}a^2 - \frac{4}{3}ab + \frac{1}{2}b^2$.
8. $48a^7b^6c^7$.
9. $\frac{16}{81}x^4y^8z^{12}$.

10. $2x^2 - 8x + 26$.

11. $8a^6b^3 - 36a^4b^2xy + 54a^2bx^2y^2 - 27x^3y^3$.

12. $x^3 - 3x^2 + 2y - 6$.

13. $x^6 - 3x^4y^2 + 3x^2y^4 - y^6$.

14. $x^4 - 1$.

15. $x^4 - y^4$.

16. $176\frac{1}{2}$ lbs.; $140\frac{1}{2}$ lbs.

17. watch, \$200; chain, \$150.

18. $2x + 4$.

19. $8\,ay$.

20. $1 + \frac{2}{3}b + \frac{1}{9}b^2 - \frac{1}{4}a^2$.

Exercise 24.

1. $5xy$.

2. $13ab$.

3. $3a^2$.

4. $5x^2y^3$.

5. $-17x$.

6. $-11x^3y$.

7. $4xz^2$.

8. $9a^2c^2$.

9. $2a^2b^3$.

10. $-3x^2y$.

11. $-5x^3y^3$.

12. $-5a^2c^4$.

13. $\frac{4}{5}x^3y$.

14. $-3a^3m^3$.

15. $8m^3x^4$.

16. $-6x^2y^2z^3$.

17. $2(x+y)^2z^2$.

18. $5(a-b)^2x$.

19. $\frac{1}{2}x^3y^3z^2$.

20. $-\frac{1}{3}a^2b^3$.

21. $x^9y^6 - 9x^7y^5 + 27x^5y^4 - 27x^3y^3$.

22. $\frac{b}{2a}$ miles.

23. $\frac{8y}{x}$ days.

24. $\frac{ab}{c}$.

Exercise 25.

1. $3ab^2 - 7b + 15a^3x$.

2. $5x^2y + 3y - 9xy^3$.

3. $8x^3y^5 - 4x^2y^2 - 2y$.

4. $13a^2b - 9ab^2 + 7b$.

5. $-\frac{6}{7}a^2x^2 + \frac{3}{2}ax^3$.

6. $-\frac{1}{3}x^2 + 2y^2$.

7. $-4y^3z^3 + 3x^2y^3z^4 - xy$.

8. $20ac - 31a^2b^4c^2$.

9. $x^6 - \frac{5}{2}x^3 + \frac{1}{2}x^4 - 4x - \frac{3}{2}x^2$.

10. $8 + \frac{32}{3}y^4 - 16y^3$.

11. $\frac{2}{3}a - \frac{1}{6}b - c$.

12. $3x - 2y - 4$.

13. xy men.

14. $\frac{60x}{a}$ minutes.

15. $\frac{100b}{x}$ apples.

Exercise 26.

1. $x - 7$.
2. $x - 3$.
3. $x^2 + 5$.
4. $y^2 - 6$.
5. $x^2 - 5x - 3$.
6. $a^2 + 2a - 4$.
7. $x^2 + xy + y^2$.
8. $a^2 - ab + b^2$.
9. $8a^3 + 12a^2b + 18ab^2 + 27b^3$.
10. $27x^5 + 9x^4y + 3x^2y^2 + y^3$.
11. $x^3 + x^2y + 3xy^2 + 4y^3$.
12. $a^3 + 4a^2b - 3ab^2 - 2b^3$.
13. $x^4 + 2x^2 - 3x + 1$.
14. $x^3 - 3x^2 + x - 1$.
15. $a^2 - a - 1$.
16. $x^4 - x^3 - x^2$.
17. $a^8 + a^5 + a^2$.
18. $a^10 - a^8 + a^6 - a^4$.
19. $x^2 + 2xy + 2y^2$.
20. $2a^2 - 6ab + 9b^2$.
21. $\frac{1}{2}x^2 + xy - \frac{1}{3}y^2$.
22. $\frac{1}{3}x^2 - \frac{1}{2}xy + \frac{2}{3}y^2$.
23. $\frac{1}{2}(x-y)^3 - (x-y)^2 - \frac{1}{4}(x-y)$.
24. $2x^2 - 3y$.
25. $4x^3 - 4x^2 - 6x + 6$.
26. $2a^3 + a^2b - 2ab^2 - b^3$.
27. $a^4 + a^2b^2 + b^4$.

28. $x^4 + x^2y^2 + y^4$.

29. $3a^3 + 2b^2$.

30. $1 + 2x - 2x^2 + 2x^3 -$ etc.

31. $1 - a - a^2 - a^3 -$ etc.

32. $2 + \frac{3}{2}a + \frac{3}{4}a^2 + \frac{3}{8}a^3 +$ etc.

33. $3 - \frac{4}{3}x + \frac{4}{9}x^2 - \frac{4}{27}x^3 +$ etc.

34. $\frac{x}{5}$ hrs.

35. $\frac{x + my + bc}{n}$ dols.

36. $\frac{am + bp}{m + p}$ cts.

37. $y - 11$ yrs.

Exercise 27.

1. $4ab^3$.
2. $3xy^2$.
3. $-2x^2y$.
4. $-2a^2b^3$.
5. $3ab^2$.
6. $3xy^3$.
7. $2x^2y$.
8. $3x^4y^3$.
9. $\frac{2}{3}m^3y^2$.
10. $\frac{(}{2})(3)a^3b^2$.
11. $-\frac{3}{4}x^3y^4$.
12. $-\frac{2}{3}ab^3$.
13. $x^2(a - b)$.
14. $a^3(x^2 + y^2)$.
15. $2ab^3\left(x^2 - y\right)^2$.

16. $4x^2y\left(m^3+y\right)^3$.

17. $\frac{3}{2}a^2b^3$.

18. $\frac{1}{2}x^2y$.

19. $10a^3b^3c^4$.

20. $4y$.

21. $15x^3y^3z^5$.

22. $5b$.

23. $\dfrac{a}{x+y}$ hrs.; $\dfrac{ax}{x+y}$ miles.; $\dfrac{ay}{x+y}$ miles.

24. 26.

25. $2(m-6)$; $2m-6$.

Exercise 28.

1. $2x-3y$.

2. x^2+5xy^3.

3. $4abc^2-7xy^2z$.

4. $\frac{1}{2}x-y^2z$.

5. $ab^3+\frac{1}{3}c^4$.

6. x^2-2x-1.

7. x^2+3x+4.

8. $2x^2-x+2$.

9. $3x^2+x-1$.

10. x^3+x^2-x+1.

11. x^3+2x^2+x-4.

12. $2x^3-x^2-3x+1$.

13. $90-x$.

14. $10x+y$.

Exercise 29.

1. $3x - y$.
2. $5x^2 - 1$.
3. $3b^2 + 4a$.
4. $x^2 - 2y^2$.
5. $1 + 3x$.
6. $1 - 7m$.
7. $4x^2 - \frac{1}{2}$.
8. $3x^3 + \frac{1}{3}$.
9. $2a^2 - a + 1$.
10. $x^3 - x^2 + x$.
11. $x^2 - x - 1$.
12. $\frac{1}{2}a^2 + 2a - 1$.
13. $4x$ in.
14. $27x^3$.
15. $4y$ ft.
16. $a - b$ miles north; $a + b$ miles.

Exercise 30.

1. 45.
2. 97.
3. 143.
4. 951.
5. 8.4.
6. .95.
7. 308.
8. .0028.
9. 3.9.
10. 73.

11. 62.3.
12. 83.9.
13. 3.28.
14. 50.5.
15. 5.898−.
16. 2.646−.
17. .501−.
18. 33 pieces.
19. 74 men.
20. 104.9+ in.
21. 92 trees.

Exercise 31.

1. $5(a^2 - 5)$
2. $16(1 + 4xy)$.
3. $2a(1 - a)$.
4. $15a^2(1 - 15a^2)$.
5. $x^2(x - 1)$.
6. $a^2(3 + a^3)$.
7. $a(a - b^2)$.
8. $a(a + b)$.
9. $2a^3(3 + a + 2a^2)$.
10. $7x(1 - x^2 + 2x^3)$.
11. $x(3x^2 - x + 1)$.
12. $a(a^2 - ay + y^2)$.
13. $(x + y)(3a + 5mb - 9d^2x)$.
14. $5(a - b)(1 - 3xy - a^2b)$.
15. $4xy(x^2 - 3xy - 2y^2)$.
16. $2axy^5(3x^2 - 2xy + y^2 - ay^4)$.

17. $17x^2y(3x^3 - 2x^2y + y^3)$.

18. $3ab(2ab - a^2b^2c - 3b^2c + c^2)$.

19. $3ax(x^6 - 8 + 3x^4 - x^3 - 3x^5)$.

20. $27a^5b^2c^3(a^3 - 3a^2b + 3ab^2 - b^3 - c^3)$.

21. $m + d + c - x$ cts.

22. 12 beads.

Exercise 32.

1. $(a + b)(x + y)$.

2. $(x + b)(x + a)$.

3. $(a - b)(x^2 + y^2)$.

4. $(x + 5)(x - a)$.

5. $(a - x)(x + b)$.

6. $(x - 4y)(x + my)$.

7. $(x^3 + 2)(2x - 1)$.

8. $(m - n)(x - a)$.

9. $(x^2 + 1)(x + 1)$.

10. $(y^2 + 1)(y - 1)$.

11. $(x^4 - x^2 + 1)(x + 1)$.

12. $(ax + by + c)(a + b)$.

13. $(a - b - c)(x - y)$.

14. $(3a - 2b)(x + y)$.

15. $(2a + 3b - c)(x - y)$.

16. $3a(2x + y)(m - n)$.

17. $250 + yA.$; $30 - x$ horses.

18. 12.

19. 70.

Exercise 33.

1. $(x + y)(x - y)$.
2. $(m + n)(m - n)$.
3. $(ab^2 + cd)(ab^2 - cd)$.
4. $(mp^2 - x^3y^2)(mp^2 + x^3y^2)$.
5. $(a^3bx^2 + m^2c^4y^{10})(a^3bx^2 - m^2c^4y^{10})$.
6. $(xy^2z^2 + cdm^2)(x^2y^2z^2 - cdm^2)$.
7. $(x^2y + a^3y^2)(x^2y - a^3y^2)$.
8. $(g^3c^3 - x^3z^4)(g^3c^3 + x^3z^4)$.
9. $(2a - 3x)(2a + 3x)$.
10. $(4m - 3n)(4m + 3n)$.
11. $(9xy^2 - 5bd)(9xy^2 - 5bd)$.
12. $(27m^2cx^5 + 100y^2)(27m^2cx^5 - 100y^2)$.
13. $(11m + 8x)(11m - 8x)$.
14. $(x^2 + y^2)(x + y)(x - y)$.
15. $(m^4 + a^4)(m^2 + a^2)(m + a)(m - a)$.
16. $(a^4b^4 + 1)(a^2b^2 + 1)(ab + 1)(ab - 1)$.
17. $(x^8 + b^8)(x^4 + b^4)(x^2 + b^2)(x + b)(x - b)$.
18. $(4a^2 + 1)(2a + 1)(2a - 1)$.
19. $a(a + x)(a - x)$.
20. $5b^2(b + a)(b - a)$.
21. $(a - b)(x + y)(x - y)$.
22. $5a(a + y)(1 + a)(1 - a)$.
23. $(m + y - a)(m - y)$.
24. $(a - x + 1)(a + x)$.
25. $x - 3y$.
26. $3x + 11$ yrs.

Exercise 34.

1. $(x+y)(x^2-xy+y^2)$.
2. $(c+d)(c^2-cd+d^2)$.
3. $(a+bc)(a^2-abc+b^2c^2)$.
4. $(ax+y)(a^2x^2-axy+y^2)$.
5. $(2abc^2+m^2)(4a^2b^2c^4-2abc^2m^2+m^4)$.
6. $(x^2y^3+6a)(x^4y^6-6ax^2y^3+36a^2)$.
7. $(a^2+b^2)(a^4-a^2b^2+b^4)$.
8. $(4x^2+y^2)(16x^4-4x^2y^2+y^4)$.
9. $(x+2)(x^2-2x+4)$.
10. $(3+ab^2)(9-3ab^2+a^2b^4)$.
11. $(y+1)(y^2-y+1)$.
12. $(1+bc^3)(1-bc^3+b^2c^5)$.
13. $(\frac{1}{2}a^2b+c^3)(\frac{1}{4}a^4b^2-\frac{1}{2}a^2bc^3+c^5)$.
14. $(\frac{1}{4}x+1)(\frac{1}{2}x^2-\frac{1}{4}x+1)$.
15. $(m+n+2)\{(m+n)^2-2(m+n)+4\}$.
16. $(1-x-y)\{1-(x-y)+(x-y)^2\}$.
17. $2a^2(xy^2+a^2b^3)(x^2y^4-a^2b^3xy^2+a^4b^6)$.
18. $(m-n)(x+y)$.
19. $(x-y)(a+b)(a^2-ab+b^2)$.
20. $(a+b)(a^2-ab+b^2)(a-b)(a^2+ab+b^2)$.
21. $(27x^3+4y^3)(27x^3-4y^3)$.
22. $(1+x^4)(1+x^2)(1+x)(1-x)$.
23. $3(d-26)$; $3d-104$ dols.
24. $10y$.
25. $x-8$.

Exercise 35.

1. $(x-a)(x^2+ax+a^2)$.
2. $(c-b)(c^2+cb+b^2)$.
3. $(a-xy)(a^2+axy+x^2y^2)$.
4. $(mn-c)(m^2n^2+mnc+c^2)$.
5. $(3m-2x)(9m^2+6mx+4x^2)$.
6. $8(x-2y)(x^2+2xy+4y^2)$.
7. $(4ax^2b-5m^3cy^2)(16a^2x^4b^2+20abcm^3x^2y^2+25m^6c^2y^4)$.
8. $27(bc^2y-2a^3m^2x^2)(b^2c^4y^2+2a^3bc^2m^2x^2y+4a^2m^4x^4)$.
9. $(2x^3y-5)(4x^6y^2+10x^3y+25)$.
10. $(3-4mx^2y)(9+12mx^2y+16m^2x^4y^2)$.
11. $(a-b^2)(a^2+ab^2+b^4)$.
12. $(m^2-x)(m^4+m^2x+x^2)$.
13. $(x-1)(x^2+x+1)$.
14. $(1-y)(1+y+y^2)$
15. $(\frac{1}{3}xy^2-b^3)(\frac{1}{9}x^3y^4+\frac{1}{3}xy^2b^3+b^6)$.
16. $(2-\frac{1}{4}m^2n)(4+\frac{1}{2}m^2n+\frac{1}{16}m^4n^2)$.
17. $\{1-(a+b)\}\{1+(a+b)+(a+b)^2\}$.
18. $\{xy-(x-y^2)\}\{x^2y^2+xy(x-y^2)+(x-y^2)^2\}$.
19. $x(x^2-y)(x^4+x^2y+y^2)$.
20. $(a+m)(b-c)(b^2+bc+c^2)$.
21. $(x+y)(x^2-xy+y^2)(x-y)(x^2+xy+y^2)$.
22. $(x^5+x^2-1)(x-1)$.
23. $(a-b)(a+b+a^2+ab+b^2)$.
24. $(x+y)(mx^2-mxy+my^2-1)$.
25. $\frac{75}{xy}$ hrs.
26. $100x+10x+y$.

Exercise 36.

1. $(a+x)^2$.
2. $(c-d)^2$.
3. $(2a+y)^2$.
4. $(a+2b)^2$.
5. $(x-3c)^2$.
6. $(4x-y)^2$.
7. $(a+1)^2$.
8. $(3-x)^2$.
9. $(x-5)^2$.
10. $(2y-3)^2$.
11. $(3x+4)^2$.
12. $(3a-1)^2(3a+1)^2$.
13. $(3c+11d)^2$.
14. $(2y-9)^2$.
15. $\left(x^2-3y\right)^2$.
16. $\left(3-2x^2\right)^2$.
17. $\left(4xy^2-3a^8\right)^2$.
18. $\left(5b+3c^2y\right)^2$.
19. $\left(7a+2x^2y\right)^2$.
20. $\left(\frac{1}{3}x^2-y^2\right)^2$.
21. $\left(\frac{1}{2}a+2b\right)^2$.
22. $\left(\frac{2}{3}x^3y-z^4\right)^2$.
23. $x^3\left(x^3-2y^4\right)^2$.
24. $2y\left(3a+2y^2\right)^2$.
25. $3ax^3\left(ax-5b\right)^2$.

26. $(x+y-a^2)^2$.

27. $\{(m^2-n^2)-(m^2+n^2)\}^2$ or $(-2n^2)^2$.

28. $(a+b)(a+b+6)$.

29. $(x-y)(x-y-3)$.

30. $(x-y)^2(x^2+xy+y^2)^2$.

31. y^2.

32. $9y^2$.

33. $\pm 2cd$.

34. 1.

35. 9.

36. $4y^4$.

37. $25y^2$.

38. $\pm 60ab^3c$.

39. $\pm 70a^2b^3cd$.

40. $16a^2$ or $28a^2$.

41. ay or $353ay$.

42. $4a^2b^2$ or $16a^2b^2$.

43. x^2 or $-3x^2$.

44. a or $-3a$.

45. $b-a$; $6(b-a)$; $b+a$; $3(b+a)$ miles.

46. $\frac{8}{15}$ of the cistern.

47. $\frac{b-9}{3}$; $\frac{b-9}{3}+9$ years.

Exercise 37.

1. $(a+2)(a+1)$.
2. $(x+6)(x+3)$.
3. $(x-3)(x-2)$.
4. $(a-5)(a-2)$.
5. $(y-8)(y-2)$.
6. $(c-3)(c+2)$.
7. $(x+5)(x-1)$.
8. $(x+6)(x-1)$.
9. $(y+13)(y-5)$.
10. $(a-11)(a+7)$.
11. $(x-9)(x+7)$.
12. $(a+15)(a-5)$.
13. $(a-11)(a-13)$.
14. $(a^3-13)(a^3+9)$.
15. $(x^3+11)(x^3-7)$.
16. $(6+x)(5+x)$.
17. $(7+a)(3+a)$.
18. $(7-x)(5-x)$, or $(x-7)(x-5)$.
19. $(9-x)(4-x)$.
20. $(c+3d)(c-d)$.
21. $(a+5x)(a+3x)$.
22. $(x-5y)(x+4y)$.
23. $(x^2+4y)(x^2-3y)$.
24. $(x^2-5y^2)(x+3y)(x-3y)$.
25. $x^3(x-12)(x-11)$.
26. $a^4(a-7)(a-5)$.
27. $3a(x+3)(x-3)(x+2)(x-2)$.

28. $3a\,(a-2b)^2$.

29. $(c-a)(c+a)(cd-1)(c^2d^2+cd+1)$.

30. $(a+b)(x-3)(x-2)$.

31. $\frac{1}{a}+\frac{1}{b}$.

32. $\frac{7x}{2}$ days.

Exercise 38.

1. $9a^2-9a-4$.
2. $3y^3+2y^2-2y-1$.
3. x^4-y^4.
4. $a^3-5a^2+26a-2$.
5. $x^6y^3-12x^4y^2z^3a^4+48x^2yz^8a^8-64z^9a^{12}$.
6. $(x-10)\,(x-1)$.
7. $(a+b+c+d)\,(a+b-c-d)$.
8. $\left(2x^2-3\right)(3x+2)$.
9. $x^4\left(3x^2-11\right)^2$.
10. $\left(2c^2-d^3\right)\left(4c^4+2c^2d^3+d^6\right)$.
11. $(1+4x)\left(1-4x+16x^2\right)$.
12. $(a+1)\left(a^2-a+1\right)(a-1)\left(a^2+a+1\right)$.
13. $(x+2)\,(x+1)\,(x-1)$.
14. $(x-y)\left(x^4+x^3y+x^2y^2+xy^3+y^4\right)$.
15. $(9+x)\,(3+x)$.
16. m^2+2m-4.
17. $-3m^2+8mn+3n^2$.
18. $52-25x-52x^2$.
19. $2x^3$.
20. 18; 19; 20.
21. 60.
22. 16.

Exercise 39.

1. $3ab^2$.
2. $5xy$.
3. $2xy^3(x+y)$.
4. $3a^2b(a-b)$.
5. $m-n$.
6. $9x^4-4$.
7. $x-5$.
8. $x+3$.
9. $a+2$.
10. $y(y-1)$.
11. $x-y$.
12. $3a\left(c^2-a^2\right)$.
13. $x^2\left(2x^3-y^2\right)$.
14. $\dfrac{ax+by}{a+b}$ cts.
15. $\dfrac{5}{100}x$ dols.
16. 5; 11.

Exercise 40.

1. $\left(a^2-4\right)(a+5)$.
2. $\left(x^3+1\right)(x+1)$.
3. $\left(x^2-9\right)(x-5)$.
4. $\left(x^6-1\right)\left(x^2-3\right)$.
5. $2\left(x^2-1\right)(x-3)(x+2)$.
6. $(a+1)^3(m-2)$.
7. $\left(a^2-4\right)\left(a^2-25\right)\left(a^2-9\right)$.
8. $(x-1)^3(y+3)$.

9. $(x^2-1)(x^2-9)(x^2-16)$.

10. $2x^3(x^3+1)(x-1)$.

11. $(1-a^4)^2$.

12. $6axz(a^2-x^2)$.

13. $(m^2-n^2)(a^2-10a+21)$.

14. $6bx(1-b^3)(1+b)$.

15. $5ab(a+x)(a-x)^2(a-x-1)$.

16. $c+y$ degrees.

17. $b-y$, or $y-b$ degrees.

18. $\frac{2}{x}$.

19. x^3+12.

20. \$ 306; \$ 1836.

Exercise 42.

1. $\dfrac{3x}{8z}$.

2. $\dfrac{2x^4}{5y}$.

3. $\dfrac{x-3}{x+5}$.

4. $\dfrac{x+6}{x-5}$.

5. $\dfrac{a^4}{a^2-1}$.

6. $\dfrac{x^2}{x^3+1}$.

7. $\dfrac{m+n}{a+2b}$.

8. $\dfrac{c+d}{x+2y}$.

9. $\dfrac{d(c-ad)}{a^2}$.

10. $\dfrac{y(a+xy)}{x}$.

11. $\dfrac{a-b}{a+b}$.

12. $\dfrac{x^2+y^2}{x^2-y^2}$.

13. $\dfrac{a(x-4)}{x+5}$.

14. $\dfrac{a^2-17}{a^2-5}$.

15. $\dfrac{1+x}{2+x}$.

16. $\dfrac{1+b}{1-b}$.

17. $\frac{2}{3}b$, or $\dfrac{2b}{3}$ cts.

18. $\dfrac{a}{x}$ years.

Exercise 43.

1. $b-c+\dfrac{m}{x}$.

2. $m+a+\dfrac{x}{n}$.

3. $x+y+\dfrac{3}{x-y}$.

4. $a^2-ab+b^2-\dfrac{2}{a+b}$.

5. $2abc-3b+\dfrac{c}{a^2b}$.

6. $3x^2+5xz-\dfrac{m}{xy^2}$.

7. $x+3+\dfrac{2x+4}{x^2-x-1}$.

8. $2a-1+\dfrac{3a-1}{a^2+a-2}$.

9. $x^2+xy+y^2+\dfrac{2y^3}{x-y}$.

10. $a^2 - ab + b^2 - \dfrac{2b^3}{a+b}$.

11. $4a^2 + 2a + 1 + \dfrac{1}{2a-1}$.

12. $9x^2 - 3x + 1 - \dfrac{1}{3x+1}$.

13. $3x + 2 - \dfrac{x-4}{x^2+2x-1}$.

14. $2a - 3 + \dfrac{15a+2}{a^2+3a+2}$.

15. $2a^2 + 4a - 2$.

16. $3x^2 - 2x + 1$.

17. $\dfrac{x^2 - y^2 - xy}{x-y}$.

18. $\dfrac{a^2 - 2ab - b^2}{a+b}$.

19. $\dfrac{2d^3}{c^2 + cd + d^2}$.

20. $\dfrac{x^3 + y^3}{x-y}$.

21. $\dfrac{4 - 4x - 3x^2}{3x-1}$.

22. $\dfrac{2a^2 + 4a - 1}{a+3}$.

23. $\dfrac{2a^4 - 6a^3 + 3a^2 + 2a - 5}{2a^2 - 1}$.

24. $\dfrac{6x^4 + 3x^3 - 7x^2 - 1}{3x^2 + 1}$.

25. $\dfrac{4x - x^2}{x^2 - x + 2}$.

26. $-\dfrac{a^2 + 2a}{a^2 - 2a + 3}$.

27. $-\dfrac{a^4 + 2a^2 + 2a + 3}{a^2 - a + 3}$.

28. $\dfrac{x^2 - 2x + 1}{x^2 + x - 1}$.

42. $\frac{m}{2x}$ ct.

43. $a-3$, $a-2$, $a-1$, a.

44. $2m+2$.

45. $4a-1$.

Exercise 44.

1. $\frac{a}{12}$.

2. $\frac{x}{15}$.

3. $\frac{43x}{60}$.

4. $\frac{4am+3bx}{2bm}$.

5. $\frac{4x}{15}$.

6. $\frac{m^4-2m^2n^2+n^4}{m^2n^2}$.

7. $\frac{3x-mx+5m^2n}{3mn}$.

8. $\frac{11b-x}{9x}$.

9. 0.

10. $\frac{2ab}{a^2-b^2}$.

11. $\frac{b^2}{(a-2b)(a-b)}$.

12. $\frac{2}{(x+5)(x+3)}$.

13. $-\frac{4y^2}{x(x-2y)}$.

14. $\frac{2x^2-4x+29}{(x+2)(x-3)}$.

15. $\frac{2ax}{x^3-8a^3}$.

16. $\dfrac{2x^9}{x^6 - y^6}$.

17. $\dfrac{m^2 + 11}{(m-1)(m+2)(m+3)}$.

18. 0.

19. $\dfrac{2(9x^4 + 1)}{9x^4 - 1}$.

20. $\dfrac{2}{(a-2)(a-3)(a-4)}$.

21. 2.

22. $\dfrac{2}{a+3}$.

23. $\dfrac{x+25}{x^2 - x - 20}$.

24. 0.

25. $\dfrac{2}{a}$.

26. $\dfrac{x^2 + xz - yz}{(x+z)(y+z)}$.

27. 0.

28. $\dfrac{x}{y}$.

29. $\dfrac{a}{2}$.

30. $\dfrac{7x}{3}$.

31. $4x - 21$.

Exercise 45.

1. $\dfrac{2}{x+2}$.

2. $\dfrac{a}{a^2 - 9}$.

3. m^2.

4. $\dfrac{1}{2a+1}$.

5. $\dfrac{3y}{x^2+xy+y^2}$.

6. $-\dfrac{1}{3(a^2-1)}$.

7. $-\dfrac{b}{5(y^4-9b^2)}$.

8. $\dfrac{1}{(1-x)(3-x)}$.

9. $\dfrac{b}{(b-c)(a-b)}$.

10. 0.

11. 1.

12. $\dfrac{2a^2}{a^2-1}$.

13. $\dfrac{1+a-a^4}{1+a}$.

14. $\dfrac{1}{(x-2)(x-3)}$.

15. $\dfrac{43a}{b}$.

16. $\dfrac{9x}{4}$.

17. $\dfrac{mx}{5}$.

18. $\dfrac{by}{a}$.

Exercise 46.

1. $\dfrac{ax}{b^2}$.

2. $\dfrac{3a^2bc}{7x^2y}$.

3. $\dfrac{a^2}{2c^2}$.

4. $\dfrac{4abc^2}{3x}$.

5. $\dfrac{9mn}{y}$.

6. $\dfrac{3x(x-y)}{2mn}$.

7. $\dfrac{2a-b}{3x-y}$.

8. $\dfrac{x^2}{x^2+xy+y^2}$.

9. $3(x+y)^2$.

10. $\dfrac{a^2-4a-21}{a+2}$.

11. $x^2-2xy+y^2$.

12. $a^2+2ab+b^2$.

13. x.

14. c.

15. 10.

16. $5x$.

17. $24a$.

Exercise 47.

1. $\dfrac{a}{b}$.

2. $\dfrac{3m^2n}{4x^2y}$.

3. $\dfrac{3d^2}{5x}$.

4. $\dfrac{2x^2y}{3m^2n}$.

5. $\dfrac{a}{3x(c+d)}$.

6. $\dfrac{x^2-y}{2m^2n}$.

7. $\dfrac{a-b^3}{5ax^2yz}$.

8. $\dfrac{5(a+b)}{xy}$.

9. $\dfrac{1}{2m\,(m-n)^2}$.

10. $\dfrac{x+7}{x^2-7x+12}$.

11. $x+1+\dfrac{1}{3x}$.

12. $\dfrac{x^2-5x+6}{x+4}$.

13. $\dfrac{c}{12a^2x^3}$.

14. $2ac+\dfrac{3a^2c^2}{2x^2y}$.

15. $\dfrac{5y(x-y)}{8x^2z}$.

16. $\dfrac{2x}{9amn^2}$.

17. $\dfrac{29}{35}$.

18. $\dfrac{1}{2m}$.

Exercise 48.

1. $\dfrac{abz}{8cxy}$.

2. $\frac{2}{3}$.

3. 2.

4. 3.

5. $\dfrac{cd}{ab}$.

6. $\dfrac{2y}{an}$.

7. $\dfrac{x+4}{x+1}$.

8. $a+5$.

9. $\dfrac{(x^2+4x+16)(3x+2)}{x}$.

10. m^2+3m+9.

11. a.

12. $\dfrac{(x-1)^2}{2x(x+3)}$.

13. $\dfrac{(a+1)^2}{3a(a+2)}$.

14. $\dfrac{m^2n^2}{m^2-n^2}$.

15. $\dfrac{25}{y}$; $\dfrac{25}{y-4}$ dols.

16. $\dfrac{2a}{3c}$.

17. 252; 224.

Exercise 49.

1. $\dfrac{6a^2bc}{7xy^2}$.

2. $\dfrac{21ab^2y^2}{16mnz^3}$.

3. $\dfrac{16a^2z^2}{9c^2x^2}$.

4. $\dfrac{4m^2y^2}{9a^2x^2}$.

5. $\dfrac{x^2-25}{x^2+2x}$.

6. $\dfrac{(x-5)(x-6)}{(x-3)(x-3)}$.

7. $\dfrac{x-2}{x-5}$.

8. $\dfrac{a(a-7)}{a+6}$.

9. 1.

10. 1.

11. 1.

12. $\frac{x-5}{x+5}$.

13. $\frac{a}{b}$.

14. $\frac{m}{2n}$.

15. a^2.

16. $\frac{1}{4x}$.

17. 3.

18. 4.

19. $\frac{dx}{4c}$.

20. $\frac{21x^4y^2}{20abn^2}$.

Exercise 50.

1. $\frac{4x^4}{a^2b^6}$.

2. $\frac{a^3b^9}{64y^3}$

3. $-\frac{32x^5y^5}{243a^{10}m^{15}}$.

4. $\frac{x^4\left(a-b\right)^4}{81a^8b^4}$.

5. $-\frac{125x^5y^3\left(a+b^2\right)^6}{8a^3b^9\left(x^2-y\right)^9}$.

6. $-\frac{27a^3m^{12}\left(2a+3b\right)^9}{64x^6y^9\left(m-n\right)^6}$.

7. $\frac{81a^{20}x^4y^8z^{12}}{16b^4c^{16}d^{16}}$.

8. $\frac{256x^{28}y^8z^{12}}{81a^4b^{24}d^{12}}$.

9. $\frac{2ab^2}{3m^2n^3}$.

10. $\dfrac{6mn^4}{11a^2b^3}$.

11. $\dfrac{4xy^2}{3ab^3}$.

12. $-\dfrac{2xy^2}{3m^2n^3}$.

13. $-\dfrac{3x^2(a-b)^3}{4a^2b^4}$.

14. $\dfrac{2x+3y}{4x^2y^4}$.

15. $\dfrac{2x(x+y)^2}{5y^2}$.

16. $-\dfrac{3a(a-b)^2}{2b^3}$.

17. $\dfrac{x^2}{y^2}-\dfrac{a^2}{b^2}$.

18. $\dfrac{a^2}{b^2}-\dfrac{c^2}{d^2}$.

19. $6x+\frac{3abx^2y}{2mn}-\frac{a^2x}{m}$.

20. $\dfrac{2x^3}{3yz}-\dfrac{3xy}{2}+\dfrac{x^4}{m^2z^2}$.

21. $\dfrac{a^8}{b^8}-\dfrac{c^8}{d^8}$.

22. $\dfrac{x^4}{256}-\dfrac{81y^4}{625m^4}$.

23. $\dfrac{x^3}{y^3}+1$.

24. $\dfrac{a^3}{b^3}-1$.

25. $\dfrac{x^2}{y^2}-\dfrac{3a^2x}{by}+\dfrac{9a^4}{4b^2}$.

26. $\dfrac{4y^2}{c^4}+\dfrac{18y}{c^2d}+\dfrac{81}{4d^2}$.

27. $\dfrac{a^2}{b^2}-\dfrac{3a}{b}-10$.

28. $\dfrac{x^3}{y^3} - \dfrac{3ax^2}{by^2} + \dfrac{3a^2x}{b^2y} - \dfrac{a^3}{b^3}$.

29. $\left(\dfrac{x^2}{a} - \dfrac{b}{y^2}\right)\left(\dfrac{x^2}{a} + \dfrac{b}{y^2}\right)$.

30. $\left(\dfrac{a}{b^2} - \dfrac{x^4}{y}\right)\left(\dfrac{a}{b^2} + \dfrac{x^4}{y}\right)$

31. $\left(\dfrac{a^2}{m^2} + \dfrac{b^2}{x^2}\right)\left(\dfrac{a}{m} + \dfrac{b}{x}\right)\left(\dfrac{a}{m} - \dfrac{b}{x}\right)$.

32. $\left(\dfrac{2a}{y} + \dfrac{b}{c}\right)\left(\dfrac{4a^2}{y^2} - \dfrac{2ab}{cy} + \dfrac{b^2}{c^2}\right)$.

33. $\left(\dfrac{x}{3a} - \dfrac{y}{c}\right)\left(\dfrac{x^2}{9a^2} + \dfrac{xy}{3ac} + \dfrac{y^2}{c^2}\right)$.

34. $\left(\dfrac{9a^2}{b^2} + \dfrac{x^2y^2}{25z^2}\right)\left(\dfrac{3a}{b} + \dfrac{xy}{5z}\right)\left(\dfrac{3a}{b} - \dfrac{xy}{5z}\right)$.

35. $\left(\dfrac{m}{y} - 5\right)\left(\dfrac{m}{y} + 3\right)$.

36. $\left(\dfrac{x}{a} - 4\right)\left(\dfrac{x}{a} + 2\right)$.

37. $\left(\dfrac{y}{2} + \dfrac{2}{y}\right)^2$.

38. $\left(\dfrac{x}{a} - \dfrac{a}{x}\right)^2$.

39. $18a$ ft.

40. $\dfrac{a}{6}$ weeks.

Exercise 51

1. $\dfrac{b+a}{x-b}$.

2. $\dfrac{xy+a}{my-b}$.

3. $\dfrac{cx}{ac+b}$.

4. $\dfrac{x^2+x+1}{x}$.

5. $\dfrac{a+b}{ab}$.

6. $m(m^2 - m + 1)$.

7. $\frac{x^2 - yz}{ax - by}$.

8. $-\frac{d}{c}$.

9. $\frac{a+1}{a-1}$.

10. a^2.

11. $\frac{x-5}{x-3}$.

12. a.

13. $\frac{a^2+1}{2a}$.

14. 1.

15. $\frac{2}{a}$.

16. l.

17. $5y$ lbs.

18. $12y$ in.; $\frac{y}{3}$ yds.

19. $100y - x^2$ cts.

20. $\frac{lx}{m}$.

Exercise 52.

1. $3x^4 - 2x^3 - x + 5$.

2. 45; 55.

3. $x + 1$.

4. $(x^5 - 7y)^2$, $(a - b)(a^2 + ab + b^2)(a^6 + a^3b^3 + b^6)$, $3(a - 9)(a + 8)$.

5. 2.

6. $\left(\frac{4x^2}{a^2b^2} + \frac{c^2}{9y^2}\right)\left(\frac{2x}{ab} + \frac{c}{3y}\right)\left(\frac{2x}{ab} - \frac{c}{3y}\right)$.

7. $10x + y$.

8. $(a^2 - 16)(a^2 - 9)(a^2 - 4)$.

9. $\dfrac{100x}{a}$.

10. $-\dfrac{6}{x-4}$.

11. 0.

12. $\dfrac{3x}{2y}$.

13. $\dfrac{2b}{n}$.

14. 1.

15. 1.

17. $42xy$.

18. $\dfrac{2x^3}{3} - \dfrac{x^2}{4} + x - 1$.

Exercise 53.

1. $x = 2$.
2. $x = -3$.
3. $x = 19$.
4. $x = -13$.
5. $x = 2\frac{1}{2}$.
6. $x = 5\frac{1}{4}$.
7. $x = 4$.
8. $x = 6\frac{1}{5}$.
9. $x = 1$.
10. $x = 3$.
11. $x = 2$.
12. $x = 1$.
13. $x = 10\frac{3}{7}$.
14. $x = 2$.
15. $x = 1$.
16. $x = 3$.

17. $x = 4$.

18. $x = 3$.

19. $x = -3$.

20. $x = 1$.

21. $x = \frac{6}{7}$.

22. $x = \frac{3}{4}$.

23. 17; 22; 66.

24. \$ 15.

25. $28x$ fourths.

26. $\dfrac{3x}{z}$ days.

27. $x = 5\frac{1}{2}$.

28. $x = -15$.

29. $x = 48$.

30. $x = 4$.

31. $x = -5$.

32. $x = -\frac{1}{9}$.

33. $x = \frac{1}{7}$.

34. $x = 9$.

35. $x = 4$.

36. $x = 3$.

37. $x = 1$.

38. $x = 2$.

39. $x = 2$.

40. $x = 11$.

41. $x = 6$.

42. $x = 8$.

43. $\dfrac{bx}{15}$ hrs.

44. $\dfrac{5m}{100}$ dols.

45. 16; 41.

46. $\dfrac{4by}{100}$ dols.

47. $x = \dfrac{c^2}{a - b + 2c}$.

48. $x = \frac{1}{2}$.

49. $x = 3$.

50. $x = \dfrac{2b - a}{2}$.

51. $x = \dfrac{ac(a^2 + c^2)}{a + c}$.

52. $x = 0$.

53. $x = 2$.

54. $x = a + b$.

55. $x = \frac{2}{3}$.

56. $x = \frac{1}{4}$.

57. $x = 1$.

58. $x = \frac{5}{11}$.

59. $x = 2$.

60. $x = 2$.

61. $x = 4$.

62. $x = 6$.

63. $x = 1$.

64. $x = \frac{7}{17}$.

65. $x = 4$.

66. $x = -7$.

67. 26; 27; 28.

68. $6y$ years.

69. $\dfrac{6x}{a}$ men.

70. $12x + 3$.

Exercise 54.

1. 209 boys; 627 girls.
2. 184; 46; 23.
3. 16; 28 yrs
4. 36; 122.
5. S., 5; H., 11 qts.
6. 17; 22; 88.
7. 9.
8. 9 fives; 18 twos.
9. 18; 15; 25 tons.
10. 15.
11. 12 M.; 36 J.
12. 80.
13. 24.
14. 48.
15. t., 5 lbs.; m., 8 lbs.; s., 14 lbs.
16. 35; 10 yrs.
17. $2070, $920.
18. 17,042; 14,981; 15,496.
19. R., 213; J., 426.
20. 63; 64; 65.
21. 16; 28.
22. 45; 75.
23. 24; 48 yrs.
24. 2; 12 yrs.
25. J., 12 yrs.; S., 28 yrs.
26. 20 yrs.
27. A., 6 yrs.; G., 18 yrs.

28. Ed., 40 yrs.; Es., 30 yrs.

29. 6 yrs.

30. 3; 12 yrs.

31. $2x^3 - 6x^2y + 18xy^2 - 27y^3$.

33. $\dfrac{y}{x-y}$.

34. $x = 7$.

35. \$32.

36. \$13.

37. A, \$47; B, \$28; C, \$61.

38. 80 cts.

39. u., \$18; cl., \$25; h., \$9.

40. J., \$ 1.80; H., \$2.42; A., \$1.25

41. $2\frac{2}{5}$ days.

42. $5\frac{5}{11}$ days.

43. $22\frac{1}{2}$ hrs.

44. $1\frac{1}{3}$ hrs.

45. $4\frac{4}{5}$ hrs.

46. $2\frac{11}{12}$ hrs.

47. $2\frac{6}{7}$ hrs.

48. $17\frac{1}{7}$; $7\frac{1}{17}$ days.

49. $1\frac{5}{7}$ hrs.

50. $\dfrac{ab}{a+b}$ days.

51. $\dfrac{cd}{c-d}$ days.

52. $x = 1\frac{1}{2}$.

53. 1.

54. $x^8 - 13x^4 + 36$.

55. $(3a + 2b)^2$; $(3 + x)(4 + x)$; $(a - 2b)(c - 3d)$.

56. (1) $10\frac{10}{11}$ m.
(2) $27\frac{3}{11}$ m.
(3) $49\frac{1}{11}$ m.

57. (1) $27\frac{3}{11}$ m.
(2) $5\frac{5}{11}$ m.; $38\frac{2}{11}$ m.
(3) $21\frac{9}{11}$ m.; $54\frac{6}{11}$ m.

58. (1) $49\frac{1}{11}$ m.
(2) $10\frac{10}{11}$ m.
(3) $32\frac{8}{11}$ m.

59. $10\frac{10}{11}$ m., $32\frac{8}{11}$ m.

60. $16\frac{4}{11}$ m.

61. $30\frac{6}{11}$ m.

62. $5\frac{5}{11}$ m. past 12M.

63. $57\frac{9}{11}$ m.

64. 20 hrs.

65. 24 hrs.; 152 hrs

66. 35 miles.

67. $14\frac{1}{2}$ miles; $70\frac{11}{16}$ miles.

68. 24 miles.

69. 6 P.M.; 30 miles from B; $25\frac{1}{2}$ miles from A.

70. 16 sec.

71. 11 ft. by 15 ft.

72. 12 ft. by 24 ft.

73. 14 ft. by 21 ft.

74. 16 sq. ft.

75. 48 ft. by 72 ft.

76. $\left(\frac{x}{2}+\frac{yz^2}{3m^3}\right)\left(\frac{x}{2}-\frac{yz^2}{3m^3}\right)$;
$(x^2-3y)(x^4+3x^2y+9y^2)$;
$(a^8+b^8)(a^4+b^4)$ etc.;
$2c(c^2-1)^2$.

77. x^3-2x^2+4x-3.

78. $7y^3 + 15x^2y - x^3$.

79. $x(x+1)$.

80. 60 ft.

81. A, 7 days; B, 14 days; C, 28 days.

82. 9; 48.

83. 18; 74.

84. $140.

85. 24; 25.

86. A, 57 yrs.; B 33 yrs.

87. 38.

88. 300 leaps.

89. With 144 leaps.

90. After 560 leaps.

Exercise 55.

1. $x = 3$, $y = 1$.
2. $x = 4$, $y = 2$.
3. $x = 7$, $y = 6$.
4. $x = 5\frac{1}{2}$, $y = 4$.
5. $x = 1\frac{1}{2}$, $y = 3$.
6. $x = 2$, $y = 3$.
7. $x = 5$, $y = -2$.
8. $x = 2$, $y = -1$.
9. $x = -2\frac{1}{4}$, $y = -\frac{1}{8}$.
10. $x = 2\frac{1}{2}$, $y = -1\frac{1}{2}$.
11. $x = \frac{1}{2}$, $y = 1\frac{1}{3}$.
12. $x = 15$, $y = -17$.
13. $x = 12$, $y = 15$.
14. $x = 6$, $y = 18$.

15. $x = 35$, $y = -49$.

16. $x = 21$, $y = 25$.

17. $x = 3$, $y = 2$.

18. $x = \frac{1}{2}$, $y = 4$.

19. $x = 12$, $y = 15$.

20. $x = \frac{a+b}{2}$, $y = \frac{a-b}{2}$.

21. $x = 39$, $y = -56$.

22. $x = -2$, $y = -1\frac{17}{21}$.

23. $\frac{7}{24}$.

24. $\frac{11}{17}$.

25. $\frac{8}{13}$.

26. $\frac{11}{13}$.

27. 24; 62.

28. 27; 63.

29. 13; 37.

30. J., 13 yrs.; H., 19 yrs.

31. A, 36 cows; B, 24 cows.

32. tea, 54; coffee, 32.

33. corn, 61; oats, 37.

34. 12 lbs of 87 kind; 26 lbs of 29 kind.

Exercise 56.

1. $x = \pm 3$.
2. $x = \pm 2$.
3. $x = \pm 5$.
4. $x = \pm 2$.
5. $x = \pm\frac{1}{2}$.
6. $x = \pm 1$.
7. $x = \pm 7$.

8. $x = \pm 2$.

9. $x = \pm 1$.

10. $x = \pm 2$.

11. $x = \pm 2$.

12. $x = \pm 3$.

13. 12 yrs.

14. 48; 64.

15. $\frac{17}{21}$

Exercise 57.

1. $x = 3$ or -6.

2. $x = 2$ or -7.

3. $x = 9$ or -8.

4. $x = 7$ or 3.

5. $x = 8$ or 15.

6. $x = 11$ or -17.

7. $x = b$ or b.

8. $x = a$ or $3a$.

9. $x = 1$ or $-a$.

10. $x = \frac{d}{c}$ or $-\frac{b}{a}$.

11. $x = 11$ or -3.

12. $x = 6$ or 1.

13. $x = 5$ or 2.

14. $x = 6$ or 4.

15. $x = 6$ or 16.

16. $x = 2$ or -3.

17. $x = 5$ or -2.

18. $x = 0$ or 5.

19. $x = 0$ or -3.

20. $x = 3$ or 3.

21. $54\frac{6}{11}$ m.

22. J., \$18; L., \$6.

23. 3 in.

24. $7\frac{31}{47}$ days.

Exercise 58.

1. 3.

3. $x = 3$.

4. 30 hrs.

5. $x - 1$.

6. $a^2 + ab - b^2$.

7. $1 - y + 3y^2 + 2y^3$.

8. $60 - x^2 - 28x$.

9. $x = \pm 6$.

10. 1.

11. $11(a - c) - 17x^3y - 3\,(a - c)^3$.

12. $x = \frac{4b}{5}$.

13. $(x^3+3)(x-1)(x^2+x+1)$; $(a+b)(x-y)(x+y)$; $(3x+y+z)\{9x^2 - 3x(y+z) + (y+z)^2\}$.

14. $\frac{5}{11}$.

15. $a + b$.

16. $x = 5$.

17. J., 16; S., 8.

18. $\dfrac{1-y}{x}$.

19. $a^2 - 3b^2 + 3c^2$.

20. $\dfrac{xy}{a}$.

21. $a + 3x + 4y + 2b$.

22. $a^2 - \frac{3}{4}a + 1$.

23. $1\frac{7}{8}$ days.

24. $\dfrac{2a^2}{a^3 + b^3}$.

25. $(x-13)(x+4)$; $(1+a^8)(1+a^4)(1+a^2)$ etc.; $\left(a^2 + b^2 + a^2 - b^2\right)^2$; or $\left(2a^2\right)^2$.

26. $x = 36$.

27. 60; 40 yrs.

28. $x = 3$, $y = 12$.

29. $3x^4 - 2x^3 + x - 5$.

30. 2.35, 3.2.

31. $3\frac{7}{16}$.

32. $x = 0$.

33. 25; 26; 27.

34. $a(a + 2)$.

35. $\dfrac{x^2 + y^2}{x}$.

36. $\frac{3}{7}$.

37. $-\dfrac{27a^6b^3\left(m+n\right)^6}{64x^3y^9\left(a-b\right)^9}$; $\pm\dfrac{5x^2\left(a+b\right)^3}{4y^3z}$.

38. $3x^2 - 2x + 1$.

39. $\frac{1}{2}$.

40. $x = -\frac{2}{3}$, $y = -\frac{3}{4}$.

41. $(x^2 + 3)(x^2 + 2)$; $(x - 7)^2$; $(x + y + z)(x - y - z)$.

42. $\frac{1}{9}x^2y^2 + xy$.

43. $31\frac{7}{11}$ m.; $44\frac{8}{11}$ m.

44. 1.

45. $x = b$.

46. $\left(\dfrac{x^3}{y^3} + \dfrac{ab^2}{c}\right)\left(\dfrac{x^3}{y^3} - \dfrac{ab^2}{c}\right)$; $\left(\dfrac{x}{y} - 7\right)\left(\dfrac{x}{y} + 2\right)$; $\left(\dfrac{x}{y} - \dfrac{y}{x}\right)^2$.

47. $4\frac{4}{5}$ days.

48. $x = 18$, $y = 6$.

49. $1 + 6x + 12x^2 + 8x^3$; $16x^8 - 96x^6a^2b^3 + 216x^4a^4b^6 - 216x^2a^5b^9 + 81a^8b^{12}$.

50. $\dfrac{a^2 + b^2}{a^2 - b^2}$.

51. $y - x$.

52. 0.

53. 400 sq. ft.

54. $2(a^2 - 1)(a - 3)(a - 2)$.

55. $-\dfrac{2a - b}{2(2a + b)}$.

56. $x = 4$ or 4.

57. $ab(a + 2cm^2)(a^2 - 2acm^2 + c^2m^4)$; $c\,(2cx + y)^2$; $(x + 1)(x^2 - x + 1)(x - 1)(x^2 + x + 1)$.

58. $1 - x - \frac{5}{12}x^2 + \frac{1}{3}x^3 + \frac{1}{9}x^4 - \frac{1}{16}x^5$.

59. $x^2 + x + 1$.

60. $x^2 - 3xy + y^2 + \frac{9xy^3 - 6y^4}{x^2 + 2y^2 - 3xy}$.

61. $a^2 + \frac{1}{2}a^3$.

62. $x = \dfrac{2ab}{a + b}$.

63. $(x + 5)(x + 5)(x^2 + 3)$; $(4 + x^4)(2 + x^2)(2 - x^2)$; $(2a)(2b)$.

64. $3\frac{3}{4}$ days.

65. $x = 5$.

66. $\dfrac{a^3}{b^3} - \dfrac{3a^2c}{b^2d} + \dfrac{3ac^2}{bd^2} - \dfrac{c^3}{d^3}$; $\dfrac{c^3}{d^3} + 1$.

67. 24 or -3.

68. $x = 15$, $y = 14$.

69. $m - my + my^2 - my^3 +$ etc.

70. $\dfrac{5x}{3}$.

71. 4 ft.

72. $10a^2 + 19ax - 19ay + 9x^2 + 18xy + 9y^2$.

73. $\frac{3}{2}x^2 - x + \frac{2}{3}$.

74. $5x^4 + 4x^3 + 3x^2 + 2x + 1$.

75. $(a+2)(a-2)(a+5)$; $(x+y)(x^2 - xy + y^2)(x-y)(x^2 + xy + y^2)$; $2x(x^2 - 3y^2)(x+y)(x-y)$.

76. 8 hrs.

77. x.

78. $x = 2$, $y = 3$.

79. $3xy - 7b^2$.

80. $6x - 23$.